YHWH
THE LORD

YHWH
THE LORD

A STUDY OF THE INFINITE NATURE AND CHARACTER
OF GOD AS REVEALED THROUGH HIS NAMES

LAURA ACKLEY

EQUIP PRESS

Colorado Springs

YHWH, The LORD

A Study of the Infinite Nature and Character of God As Revealed Through His Names

Copyright © 2021 Laura Ackley

All rights reserved. No part of this publication may be reproduced, distributed, or transmitted in any form or by any means, without prior written permission.

Scripture quotations marked (ESV) are taken from The ESV® Bible (The Holy Bible, English Standard Version®) copyright © 2001 by Crossway, a publishing minis-try of Good News Publishers. ESV® Text Edition: 2011. The ESV® text has been reproduced in cooperation with and by permission of Good News Publishers.

Unauthorized reproduction of this publication is prohibited. Used by permission.

All rights reserved.

Scripture quotations marked (KJV) are taken from the King James Bible. Accessed on Bible Gateway at www.BibleGateway.com.

Scripture quotations marked (NASB) are taken from the New American Standard Bible® (NASB), copyright © 1960, 1962, 1963, 1968, 1971, 1972, 1973, 1975, 1977, 1995 by The Lockman Foundation, www.Lockman.org. Used by permission.

Scripture quotations marked (NIV) are taken from the Holy Bible, New International Version. Copyright © 1973, 1978, 1984, 2011 by Biblica, Inc.® Used by permission. All rights reserved worldwide.

Scripture quotations marked (NKJV) are taken from the New King James Version®. Copyright © 1982 by Thomas Nelson, Inc. Used by permission. All rights reserved.

Scripture quotations marked (NLT) are taken from the Holy Bible, New Living Translation, copyright © 1996, 2004, 2015 by Tyndale House Foundation. Used by permission of Tyndale House Publishers, Inc., Carol Stream, Illinois 60188. All rights reserved.

Scripture quotations marked (NRSV) are taken from the New Revised Standard Version Bible, copyright © 1989 the Division of Christian Education of the National

Scripture quotations taken from the Amplified® Bible (AMP), Copyright © 2015 by The Lockman Foundation Used by permission. www.Lockman.org

First Edition: 2021

YHWH, The LORD / Laura Ackley

Paperback ISBN: 978-1-951304-76-8

eBook ISBN: 978-1-951304-77-5

DEDICATION

I dedicate the Bible study, *YHWH, The LORD*, to the LORD as it was written out of love for Him with the sole purpose of bringing glory to His name.

YHWH, THE LORD: TABLE OF CONTENTS

Lesson 1: YHWH Jireh, The LORD Will Provide	13
Lesson 2: YHWH Rapha', The LORD Will Heal	38
Lesson 3: YHWH Nissi, The LORD Is My Banner	63
Lesson 4: YHWH Mekaddishkem, The LORD Our Sanctifier	89
Lesson 5: YHWH Shalom, The LORD Is Peace	115
Lesson 6: YHWH Sabaoth, The LORD of Hosts	141
Lesson 7: YHWH Tsidkenu, The LORD Our Righteousness	168
Lesson 8: YHWH Shammah, The LORD Is Present	193
Lesson 9: YHWH Raah, The LORD Is My Shepherd	219
Lesson 10: YHWH Elohim and YHWH Hoseenu, Eternal Creator and The LORD Our Maker	246

ACKNOWLEDGEMENTS

I would like to begin by thanking Dr. Darren Heil, my pastor and friend, for regularly modeling deep study of Biblical texts and increasing my desire to search out the riches within each Scripture passage I encounter. You've acted as a sounding board, provided me with honest, invaluable feedback, and encouraged me to press on as I wrote this Bible study. I'm grateful for your leadership and example in my life. To God be the glory.

Additionally, I would like to thank my amazing parents, Billy, and Beth Bennett, for supporting all of my crazy ideas, encouraging me to continually pursue after Christ, and teaching me the value of service to others for the sake of Jesus. I love you both. To God be the glory.

I would also like to thank my loving husband, Scott Ackley, for praying with me as I battled discouragement, honoring and valuing me in ministry, and selflessly sacrificing to provide me with alone time to write this Bible study. I love you. To God be the glory.

Finally, I would like to thank my Lord and Savior, YHWH. You are needless and self-sufficient in all things, but you invite imperfect people like myself to join you in the process of building your Kingdom. You do not discredit my weak attempts to honor you, however feeble they may be. You loved me first and have been faithful to me all of the days of my life. I'm unworthy to know you, but you call me your friend. You are the absolute joy and prize of my life. I love you.

FORWARD/INTRODUCTION

This Bible study is designed for individuals or groups that have the desire to seek out and know the person of God. *YHWH, The LORD*, is not designed to be a self-help, human-centered, life-application Bible study; rather, the entire focus is upon the person of YHWH and unearthing truths about His uncreated, unchanging, inexhaustible, self-sustaining, personal, and eternal attributes. This Bible study devotes two weeks of study to each compound name of God. The design of this Bible study includes commentary to read and study questions to answer each Monday through Thursday as readers are led through a thorough analysis of Biblical texts. On Fridays, the content of the Bible study includes reflection questions and activities based upon the Scriptures studied throughout the week. Although the names of God are found in the Old Testament, this Bible study leads readers through both Old Testament and New Testament passages to provide readers with a comprehensive understanding of the infinite and unchanging aspects of the LORD's character as revealed through His names.

Before studying God according to His Word, it is important to understand the names used for God in the Bible. The Hebrew name "Elohim" is translated in English as "God." This name is often used to express God's sovereign power as both the Creator and Ruler of all. Another name ascribed to God is "Adonai." This name is translated as "Lord" and points to His leadership and supreme authority. There is another name assigned to God, and it will be the focus of this Bible study. It is four letters, known as the tetragrammaton, in the biblical-age Hebrew: YHWH. In English, "YHWH," is translated as "LORD." YHWH was used throughout the Old Testament, but it wasn't until the LORD appeared to Moses in the burning bush and revealed Himself to be "I AM WHO I AM" that God's personal name was understood to represent the uncreated, unchanging, inexhaustible, self-sustaining, personal, eternal God in all of His fullness (Exod. 3:1-15).[1] Both "I AM" and "YHWH" are formed from the Hebrew word "hayah," which means "to be." We

---

1 *ESV Study Bible: English Standard Version*. Wheaton, IL: Crossway, 2011.

find that "I AM" and "YHWH" are used interchangeably in Exodus 3:14-15 when God revealed His personal name to Moses through the burning bush. Many belonging to the Jewish and Christian faiths consider God's personal name so holy that they do not speak "YHWH" for fear of mispronunciation and lack-of-reverence for the person of God. It is from attempts to pronounce God's personal name, YHWH, that the man-made words "Jehovah" and Yahweh" have arisen. While "Elohim" and "Adonai" could be used to describe a generic deity figure, God's proper Hebrew name, "YHWH," reveals that He is a being with unique character and personhood.

This 20-week Bible study focuses on Scripture surrounding ten different names ascribed to YHWH throughout the Old Testament: the LORD Will Provide, the LORD Our Healer, the LORD Our Banner, the LORD Our Sanctifier, the LORD Our Peace, the LORD Our Righteousness, the LORD of Hosts, the LORD Is Present, the LORD Is My Shepherd, and the LORD Our Maker/ the Eternal Creator. To attach a word to the LORD's personal name would be to describe an infinite, unchanging aspect of the nature and character of the eternal LORD Himself. As we embark upon a study of His nature, the goal is that we will consequently worship and love the LORD rather than a false image of God. When Jesus was asked about the greatest commandment, He responded that it was to "love the Lord your God with all your heart and with all your soul and with all your mind" (Matt. 22:37). We cannot love God with all of our hearts, souls, and minds without knowing Him rightly. Thankfully, due to His unending grace, He has revealed Himself to mankind through His inspired Scripture and Jesus, who is the Word made flesh (John 1:14) — the exact representation of the Father (Col. 1:15). As we study the God of the Bible, we come to know Him rather than an idol. As we find God and mediate upon His nature, He cultivates love within our hearts for Himself.

To love YHWH is to refuse to create our own versions of God based upon finite human thinking. As the Israelites, God's chosen people, embraced a covenant relationship with God, God provided them with ten commandments to explain how Israel would manifest their faithfulness and love to Himself. The first commandment given required that God's people behave exclusively loyal to Himself as the one and only true God:

"You shall have no other gods before me" (Exod. 20:3). The second commandment given ensured that God would not be represented by manmade means and prohibited the people from worshipping aspects of His creation or their own crafted gods: "You shall not make for yourself a carved image, or any likeness of anything that is in heaven above, or that is in the earth beneath, or that is in the water under the earth. You shall not bow down to them or serve them …" (Exod. 20:4-5a). Regardless of good intentions, if we focus on the LORD's characteristics that we enjoy while neglecting attributes of God that are difficult to understand or believe, we fabricate and worship false images of God Almighty and bow down to idols of our own making. It is human nature to exchange the glory of the immortal God for images resembling mortal man and other aspects of creation (Rom. 1:23); therefore, those who seek to know and honor God must actively search out the riches of His character and nature. Christians must guard against exchanging the truth about God for a manmade version of God that is nothing less than a lie (Rom. 1:25).

As you study YHWH's nature as the LORD Will Provide, the LORD Our Healer, the LORD Our Banner, the LORD Our Sanctifier, the LORD Our Peace, the LORD Our Righteousness, the LORD of Hosts, the LORD Is Present, the LORD Is My Shepherd, and the LORD Our Maker/ the Eternal Creator, ask the LORD to help you know the unsearchable, infinite God. Ask God to deliver you from the temptation to become satisfied with your current understanding of the Inexhaustible. Commit to searching out the depths of His personhood rather than settling for half-truths that keep you comfortable. He is holier and worthier than we could even begin to imagine, yet if it is your desire to know the LORD, He promises, "You will seek me and find me, when you seek me with all your heart" (Jer. 29:13). Seek YHWH. Find YHWH. Grow in your love for YHWH.

LESSON 1: YHWH JIREH, THE LORD WILL PROVIDE

In the Garden of Eden, God provided everything from the breath of life to the mist coming up from the ground to water the earth (Gen. 2:6). His design ensured that His creation had every resource available to multiply and thrive, and the intricacies of creation reveal the nature of God as He richly provides for every living thing and sustains all things by His powerful word (Heb. 1:3). Though they daily experienced the provision of God Almighty in the Garden, Adam and Eve were quick to forget their Provider. They were deceived by Satan into thinking that there was something that they lacked — something good that God had withheld from them. Because Provider is a divine attribute of God, God continued to provide for Adam and Eve despite their sin and rebellion against Himself. God spilt animal blood to provide animal skin as clothing for Adam and Eve, which foreshadowed the coming sacrificial system for the forgiveness of sins and the greatest provision of God — the sacrifice of Jesus as atonement for the sins of the world (Gen. 3:21). Additionally, throughout the Scriptures, God provided promises and fulfilled them. He raised up judges, deliverers, kings, and prophets to provide direction and stability to His people. From cover to cover of the Word of God, we see countless acts of provision that prove His identity — YHWH Jireh: The LORD Will Provide.

Since God is Provider, mankind is by nature the ones for which God has provided. Men and women work and strive trying to accumulate possessions, wealth, power, goodness, and fame as a means of providing for themselves as they desperately try to make themselves whole and complete. Adam and Eve were deceived into believing that God had withheld something good from them; therefore, they ate of the forbidden fruit in hopes of providing themselves with god-like wisdom (Gen. 3:6). The same enemy that was in the Garden continues to try and convince us that God cannot be trusted to take care of us. He whispers convincing lies and twists Scripture as He tries to make men and women believe that the Provider withholds good things. If we allow these lies to take root in our hearts, we will vainly attempt to provide for ourselves what only God can provide. As we seek to be our own provider, we exalt ourselves as the ones who make success, build happiness, and accomplish provision. Our controlling actions, however unintentional, spit in the face of God: "I don't need you." We will never be able to provide for ourselves because it is only in Him that "all things hold together" (Col. 1:17). It is only in understanding deeply who God is as our Provider that we become free from the anxiety of trying to step into God's role as the Provider of our lives. Trusting in God as Provider is an act of humility and surrender to His Headship.

Throughout the next two weeks, we will study a name that Abraham ascribed to God as he named the mount on which he was asked to sacrifice Isaac, YHWH Jireh. It was on this mountain that God provided a ram caught in the thicket nearby to be offered in the place of Isaac. Abraham's willingness to carry out the act of offering up His son, the one through which God has promised to provide countless descendants, proved that he believed that the LORD was the provider of fulfilled promises. In attaching a word to God's personal name, YHWH, Abraham was describing an infinite, unchanging, eternal characteristic of God's nature. When Abraham attaches "jireh" to the LORD's name, he is declaring a divine attribute of God. The word "jireh," or "yireh," is translated to English as "will provide." In short, "YHWH Jireh" is translated to "the LORD Will Provide." As you study this week, remember that God's provision is tied to His Holy Name. He will not fail as Provider because He cannot deny Himself. Ask God to personally reveal Himself to you through His Word so that you can better know the unsearchable and incomprehensible God.

MONDAY AND TUESDAY (DAY 1 AND 2): GOD PROVIDES THE PROMISE

Do you know what it is like to desperately long for something? Do you know what it's like to pray for the same thing for many years? In a culture that placed great worth on one's ability to have children, Abram and Sarai were without an heir. Abram was 75 years old when God first spoke to him about his future offspring, but Isaac was not born until Abraham was 100 years old (Gen. 21:5). Abram and Sarai had to wait upon the LORD for 25 years before the promise of God was fulfilled. Although the timing of God may not always make sense on this side of Heaven, we can trust that YHWH's plan is good (Jer. 29:11). He can be trusted to keep His promises. Even in the waiting and the disappointment, the LORD is providing exactly what is needed to produce the most fruit in the lives of believers. His provision is carried out according to His flawless timetable and for His glory. We can say alongside the psalmist: "I wait for the Lord, my soul waits, and in His Word I hope" (Ps. 130:5) because "we know that for those who love God all things work together for good, for those who are called according to His purpose" (Rom. 8:28). YHWH Jireh will provide what is necessary to fulfill His promises.

Throughout the next two days, carefully read the outlined Scripture passages from the book of Genesis in order to deepen your understanding of the context of the "YHWH Jireh" passage before studying the only mention of YHWH Jireh (The LORD Will Provide) in the Bible. Then, answer the questions thoughtfully and prayerfully. As you study YHWH, ask God to reveal His nature to you.

READ GENESIS 12:1-7.
In your own words, what command did the LORD give Abram?

What did the LORD promise Abram?

What sacrifices did Abram have to make in order to obey the word of the LORD?

Have you ever been led to sacrifice something to act in obedience to God's Word? If so, describe your experience.

READ GENESIS 15:1-6.
What trial was Abram experiencing?

Describe the illustration that the LORD used to describe His provision for Abram in light of Abram's trial.

What trials are you experiencing in which you need to recognize your need for God's provision?

READ GENESIS 16: 1-4.
What events occurred in these verses?

Do you think that Sarai's plan indicates that she trusts in God or herself as her Provider? Explain.

READ GENESIS 16:12.
Describe Ishmael.

What were the consequences of Abram and Sarai's actions?

Have you ever tried to take matters into your own hands instead of trusting the Provider? What were the results?

Note: In Genesis 17, Abram's name is changed to Abraham and Sarai's name is changed to Sarah.

READ GENESIS 18:9-15.

Why do you think Sarah laughed?

When would Sarah have a son?

Can you think of a time in which you struggled with trusting God's provision as you dwelt on your circumstances? Explain.

READ GENESIS 21:1-7.
What occurred in this passage?

> Describe the emotions you think Abraham and
> Sarah experienced and explain your answer.

Abram sacrificed greatly in leaving behind his country, family, and stability in order to obey the LORD. He stepped out in faith, leaving behind human means of support, and clung to the promise that he would become a great nation. Coming from a family that worshipped other gods (Josh. 24:2), it is striking that Abram was chosen by God to receive this blessing and become a blessing to the world. It would be through Abraham's line that the promised Messiah would be provided for the atonement of sins. This is a great reminder that God does not need our credentials or "good" behavior in order to use us for His mighty purposes. Surely, after Abram was chosen by the LORD and the LORD had manifested Himself to Abram, Abram was greatly encouraged. Yet, as time passed, Sarai was found to be barren. Delay has a way of amplifying our sinful desires for control and often reveals our lack of faith in the sovereignty of the LORD.

After Abram expressed his concerns regarding his lack of an heir, the LORD provided him with an object lesson: "Look toward heaven, and number the stars, if you are able to number them… so shall your offspring be" (Gen. 15:5). In God's mercy, every time Abram looked at the stars, their vast numbers would serve as a reminder of the promises of the LORD. As time passed, Sarai and Abram grew impatient. They doubted the miraculous power of God to provide the son of promise; therefore, they took matters into their own hands and Abram slept with Sarai's servant, Hagar, at his wife's request. Hagar became pregnant with Abram's first son. Their feeble attempts to provide for themselves resulted in heartache and conflict rather than the happiness that sin deceptively promised. Sarai and Abram's attempts to make God's plan come about resulted in lasting consequences, as Ishmael's descendants still engage in conflict with Isaac's descendants today. The LORD allowed Abram and Sarai to go through with their plan and reap the consequences as they experienced the sanctifying truth: They are powerless to provide for themselves in their own strength. They are in need of YHWH Jireh.

After the LORD changed Abram and Sarai's names to Abraham and Sarah, God ordained that Sarah would hear for herself the plan of God. This is fitting because "faith comes from hearing" (Rom. 10:17), and Sarah needed an increase in faith. Although Sarah doubted and laughed at the idea of bringing a child into the world in her old age, the LORD remained faithful to His word and asked a question that should ring in our hearts in the face of our doubts: "Is anything too hard for the LORD" (Gen. 18:14)? Proving that nothing is impossible with the LORD, Sarah did in fact bear a son, Isaac. As Abraham and Sarah learned to do throughout their faith-journey, we must regularly cling to YHWH Jireh and battle the temptation to trust in ourselves and our own means of providing.

In application, we must recognize that we are prone to become impatient, doubt God's ability to provide, and seek to provide for ourselves. In our pride, we are prone to want what we want exactly when we want it. We are prone to spiral into negative thought processes that question the perfect plan of God. Of course, the LORD could have provided an heir to Abram immediately, but the LORD is committed to the sanctification of His people; He is committed to pruning and refining their hearts like gold. The LORD is committed to exposing our sin and lack of faith to lead us to repentance and freedom. We must cling to the truth that "the Lord is not slow to fulfill His promise as some count slowness, but is patient toward [us] ..." (2 Pet. 3:9). When our circumstances do not align with our expectations, we are often tempted to assume the role that belongs to God. Put simply, it is an act of treason against God whenever we attempt to sit on His throne and exalt ourselves as the god of our lives. Whenever we exhibit impatience, we indicate with our actions that we do not trust YHWH Jireh and believe that we would perform better as provider. Today, confess your sins and receive forgiveness from the only one able to provide the forgiveness of sins.

WEDNESDAY AND THURSDAY (DAY 3 AND 4): THE LORD WILL PROVIDE

Trusting in God as Provider does not mean that we wait idly for the LORD to move mountains for His purposes. Do you often find yourself idle? There is responsibility given to us by God in order that we might show our love to God through obedience to His commands (John 14:15). Often, His commands require radical obedience and child-like faith in His character. It is unlikely that we will understand His good and perfect plan while experiencing a trial or faith-test. If we could see the upcoming breakthrough and God-ordained outcome in the midst of our situation, it would arguably be easier to trust that the LORD Will Provide. In His grace, God chooses to allow trials and faith tests in our lives because they produce what is needed within us to persevere in Christ. One thing is sure, despite our lack of understanding: God can be trusted to keep His Word and stay true to His nature as Provider. The LORD Will Provide is His name!

Over the next two days, carefully read Genesis 22, which contains the only mention of YHWH Jireh (the LORD Will Provide) in the Bible and answer the questions thoughtfully and prayerfully. You will find that YHWH Jireh's name focuses on God's provision of a lamb, which foreshadows the sacrificial death of Jesus. Although God does provide in other ways for His people, His name is directly tied to the provision of the Sacrificial Lamb. When asked to focus upon YHWH's character as provider, it is a temptation to become self-centered and tie His name to lesser aspects of life: the provision of cars, raises, jobs, etc. As you read, ask the Holy Spirit to convict you and correct your thinking about YHWH Jireh.

READ GENESIS 22:1-8.
What did God command Abraham to do?

What was Abraham's response? Why do you think Abraham responded that way?

How did Isaac respond to the events that took place in these verses? What does his response suggest?

READ HEBREWS 11:17-19.
How do these verses help make sense of Abraham's words in Gen. 22:5 and 22:8?

Have you ever experienced a time in which God helped you respond to a difficult situation in a way that was contrary to your nature? If so, explain.

READ GENESIS 22:9-14.

How can you describe the relationships between Abraham and God and between Abraham and Isaac?

What did God do to intervene and stop Abraham from sacrificing Isaac?

Why is the name that Abraham gave the place of sacrifice significant? What do you think Abraham meant by this name?

Special Note: In Hebrew, YHWH Jireh also means "The LORD sees."

Explain the connection between the LORD's seeing and provision.

READ GENESIS 22:15-19.
Who does the LORD swear by? What type of meaning does this give the LORD's promise?

In your own words, what is Abraham's reward for his obedience?

In light of John 14:15, how would you describe Abraham's relationship with God?

Note: In these verses, Isaac is described as Abraham's "only son." We know that Abraham had another son, Ishmael, by Sarai's servant Hagar according to Genesis 16. We know that Ishmael and Hagar were sent away by Abraham in Genesis 21.

RE-READ GENESIS 22:2, 12, 16.
Why do you think God used the language "only son" when speaking of Isaac? (See also, John 3:16 and Rom. 8:32.)

In Genesis 22, God commands a loving father to perform an excruciating task — God commands Abraham to sacrifice his beloved son. God's command is surprising, but more surprising is the level of commitment that Abraham exhibited to the LORD. Without delay, Abraham prepared for the journey and upcoming sacrifice and headed toward the place in which God had directed. At this place, he faithfully followed through with the command of God until the LORD stopped him right before he slaughtered Isaac. YHWH Jireh provided a ram as a substitute and the principal of substitutionary atonement was displayed. Jesus, the Lamb of God, would later die the substitutionary sacrificial death on the cross for the sins of the world (John 1:29). YHWH Jireh was faithful to provide the substitute ram for Isaac just as He was faithful in providing Jesus as the atoning sacrifice to spare believers from the wrath of God.

Abraham steadfastly obeyed God despite the pain he certainly felt in his heart. Abraham's past experiences with God had taught him that God was faithful and able to keep His promises. Abraham knew that God had promised that Isaac would be the one through which all the nations of the world would be blessed. Abraham had faith that God would have to perform the first resurrection in the Bible in order to keep His promises. He was willing to obey YHWH because "he considered that God was able even to raise him from the dead" (Heb. 11:19). Abraham's displayed faith was evidenced by works. His faith became a model for all of Israel; they were to believe God to the point of obedience. Abraham's faith is the kind of faith that is evidenced by works that will cause one to be saved and counted as righteous in the sight of YHWH (James 2:22-23).

As you reflect upon this passage, take an honest look at your life. Are you quick to obey God even when you do not understand His commands? Your level of obedience to the LORD reveals your level of trust in the Almighty Provider. Your obedience to God shows your love for God or the lack thereof. Secondly, how convinced are you that the promises of God are true? Remember, Abraham was commended as righteous due to his faith in God. If you recognize that your faith is lacking, let your prayer be like the desperate father who had brought his son to Jesus for deliverance from an unclean spirit: "I believe; help my unbelief" (Mark 9:24).

FRIDAY (DAY 5): REFLECTION

After this week of studying YHWH Jireh, the LORD Will Provide, take time to reflect on your level of obedience to the commands and leadership of God.

In what ways do you need to practice obedience to God and submit to His leadership in your life today?

Write a prayer asking God to forgive you for rebelling against His leadership in your life. Then, list three ways in which you can practically submit to the LORD's authority in your life.

MONDAY AND TUESDAY (DAY 6 AND 7): THE LORD PROVIDES THE LAMB

Over the next two days, you will be diving into Scripture regarding God's provision for right-standing with God and atonement for our sin. YHWH Jireh's provision is perfect and complete: "God will supply every need of yours according to his riches in glory in Christ Jesus" (Phil. 4:19). Often, we limit our thinking of God's provision to the acts that meet our daily needs (Matt. 6:31-32), and we neglect to focus our attention on Jesus Christ, who left Heaven to take on human form, live a perfect life (Heb. 4:15), and die the death that our sins demand.

In Jesus, we see God's greatest two-fold act of provision for all who believe. First, Jesus provides us with His substitutionary death as He gave up His life as a ransom for ours (Rev. 5:9). Secondly, Christians are not just accredited with Jesus' death, they are also accredited with Jesus' perfectly righteous life. When someone is born again into God's kingdom, he or she receives Jesus' imputed righteousness in replacement for his or her rebellious life against God. That is how a believer is able to able to declare that they have "become the righteousness of God" in Christ (2 Cor. 5:21). As Satan seeks to tempt us toward self-pity whenever we lack certain comforts on the earth, we must align our hearts with the truth that YHWH has already provided for us in Jesus. "He who did not spare His own Son but gave Him up for us all, how will He not also with Him graciously give us all things (Rom. 8:32)? If you find yourself questioning the provision of YHWH in your life, look to Jesus! Thank The LORD Will Provide today for Jesus.

RE-READ GENESIS 22:8, 13-14.
Rewrite the verses in your own words.

READ ROMANS 3:10-18, 3:23.
What type of picture do these verses paint in regard to mankind?

According to Romans 6:23, what is the just punishment from the Holy God for our rebellion against Him?

READ ROMANS 5:6-11 AND 1 JOHN 4:10.
What were the actions of Jesus Christ according to these verses?

Why did God send Jesus as a propitiation (atoning sacrifice) for our sins?

READ JOHN 1:29-30.
How does John the Baptist describe Jesus?

What do you think that John meant
by his description of Jesus?

CHOOSE TWO OF THE FOLLOWING VERSES: JOHN 3:16, EPHESIANS 1:7, AND 1 PETER 3:18.
How does God's provision for Abraham
relate to God's provision for us in Jesus?

READ 1 JOHN 2:2 AND HEBREWS 2:17.
In your own words, explain what it means that Jesus
was our propitiation. Use a dictionary if needed.

READ 2 CORINTHIANS 5:21.
What did God impute upon Christ?

What did God impute upon us?

READ ROMANS 5:18, 1 CORINTHIANS 1:30, AND ISAIAH 53:11.
Through Jesus' perfect life, what else was provided to us in Christ?

While we were dead in our sins, rebels guilty of high treason, and haters of God, Christ died the death that we deserved. Since our depraved state separated us from God, a spotless sacrifice was required in order for forgiveness to occur. Without the shedding of blood, there is no forgiveness (Heb. 9:22). Due to our sinful nature, we were powerless to save ourselves, yet the justice of God demanded the blood of a perfect and spotless Lamb. Jesus accomplished what we were powerless to do; He brought about our salvation by dying on the cross in our place according to the will of God. Though Jesus was sent by God and in submission to God, Jesus willingly chose to lay down His life for His own. In John 10:18, His will was recorded: "No one takes [my life] from me, but I lay it down on my own accord. I have authority to lay it down, and I have authority to take it up again." This act shows us the depths of His love: "While we were still sinners, Christ died for us" (Rom. 5:8).

In addition to Jesus' death, we are also provided with His righteous life. Every act that Jesus performed on the earth was to fulfill all righteousness (Matt. 5:13). As Jesus became sin though He had never sinned, we who are in Christ become the righteousness of God though all of our righteous acts only amount to filthy rags (2 Cor. 5:21, Isa. 64:6). YHWH Jireh provided the sacrifice needed to satisfy God's holy wrath against sin and provided us with His righteousness. In response, we must repent of our sins and believe in the Gospel of Jesus Christ. As we meditate on the LORD's greatest acts of Provision, our only response is to thank YHWH Jireh for the provision of Jesus' death and life for all who will believe! Christians need the Good News studied in the previous passages every day as they seek to live righteously while continually battling their sinful flesh. When you are feeling condemned for your sins, remember that if you are in Christ, the condemnation that you deserved was poured out on Jesus (Rom. 8:1). Ask the LORD Will Provide to help you preach the Good News of Jesus' provision to yourself and others every day.

WEDNESDAY AND THURSDAY (DAY 8 AND 9): PROVIDER OF DAILY NEEDS

YHWH Jireh will never act contrary to His character as Provider. As those provided for, we do not deserve His care and provision; therefore, thankfulness should characterize our lives despite our circumstances. It is YHWH's will that His people give thanks in all circumstances (1 Thess. 5:18) because if we do not cultivate a thankful heart for the food, clothing, shelter, rain, and other blessings God faithfully provides, we lose sight of the fact that without God's daily provision we would be utterly ruined. The very air we breathe, the rotation of the earth, the sun, the water cycle, etc., all point to the LORD Will Provide, yet we are so prone to take His acts of provision for granted. When we do not receive what we want from the Provider on our timetable, we are tempted to spiral downward into a pit of self-pity. This selfishness can be battled by recounting the many acts of YHWH's provision that we experience moment by moment.

God's acts of provision are not limited to our basic survival needs. When one is in Christ, he or she is adopted as His son or daughter (Eph. 3:20), counted as a friend of God (John 15:15), and created for good works (Eph. 2:10). According to YHWH's character, we are provided with a family, friendship, a sense of belonging, love, and a mission while on the earth. He provides all that we need to live lives of godliness and equips us for every good work. In light of these amazing truths, the LORD expects His people to live lives of obedience to Himself without grumbling or questioning His leadership when we find ourselves in the midst of unpleasant circumstances. Through putting off grumbling and putting on an attitude of thanksgiving, the people of God shine as lights during a crooked, dark generation (Phil. 2:14-16). As you study YHWH Jireh's daily provision, ask the LORD to reveal areas in your life in which you should take-up a thankful attitude and put-off self-pity, grumbling, and complaining. Your words are heard by YHWH Jireh and reveal your level of trust in the person of YHWH. "On the day of judgment people will give account for every careless word they [spoke]" (Matt. 12:36). Pray that the LORD will "set a guard ... over [your] mouth" and "keep watch over the door of [your] lips" so that you do not speak against the Provider (Psa. 141:3).

READ LUKE 12:22-31.
In what specific ways does God promise to provide?

What illustrations does Jesus use to communicate his provision?

How do these illustrations relate to your life?

Instead of being anxious about your life,
what should you fix your attention on?

Practically, what does it look like for
you to "seek His Kingdom?"

READ PHILIPPIANS 4:19, PSALM 23:1, AND PSALM 34:10.
What do these verses indicate about
the character of God?

READ HEBREWS 13:20-21 AND EPHESIANS 2:10.
In what way does God provide for you in ministry?

READ 2 TIMOTHY 3:16-17.
How do these verses encourage you?

READ HEBREWS 13:5.
What promise does God make?

How might faith in the promise of God help one obey the command of God in this verse?

In what area of your life do you need to trust in YHWH Jireh more?

What steps could you take to demonstrate your trust in God's provision?

Although Jesus makes it clear that He cares deeply about providing for His children, it is important to humbly confess that His ways are higher than our ways (Isa. 55:9). YHWH Jireh, whose character is to supply our every need according to His glorious riches (Phil. 4:19), does not always carry out His provision according to our expectations. Consider the Israelites as they traveled through the desert. God supernaturally provided them with manna, quail, and water, but they grumbled against YHWH because His provision did not match their standards (Exod. 16:8). Instead of adopting a sinful mindset that accuses the LORD Will Provide of falling short on His job, we must obey the LORD's command to "give thanks in all circumstances" (1 Thess. 5:18). We must guard our hearts against complaining and murmuring against Him because thankfulness is our daily worship to The LORD Will Provide. If there is something that the LORD's people truly need, will He not provide it?

Additionally, YHWH Jireh's provision stretches far beyond our basic needs. God provides us with access to Himself. According to Jeremiah 29:13-14a, the LORD says: "You will seek me and find me, when you seek me with all of your heart. I will be found by you…" Food, clothing, jobs, friends, family members, and other blessings in life do not compare to the provision of being able to know YHWH. He provides His infallible Word to us so that we can grow in our knowledge of who YHWH is and equips us for a life committed to honoring Jesus as LORD. As many who don't follow Jesus flounder and struggle to find meaning in life, YHWH provides His own with adoption as sons and daughters and gives them a mission while on earth. If we take an honest look at our lives, we will find the LORD's perfect provision at every turn. Though we are entitled to nothing and are unworthy to serve such a holy God, the saints that fear Him have no lack (Ps. 34:9). Today, don't let your heart remain hard against your Provider; rather, praise YHWH Jireh for His acts of provision that you might not have recognized before. Ask YHWH to help you regularly acknowledge His manifested character as Provider in your day-to-day life.

FRIDAY (DAY 10): REFLECTION

After this week of studying "YHWH Jireh, The LORD Will Provide," take time to reflect upon the LORD's Provision in your life. Take time to write a prayer of thanksgiving to Jesus for His provision in your life.

In what specific ways has God provided for you? Which ways mean the most to you? Explain your answer.

Write your prayer of thanksgiving.

In what areas are you prone to complain against YHWH Jireh? What Scripture can you memorize to help you combat the sins of complaining, grumbling, and ungratefulness?

Write a prayer of repentance.

LESSON 2: YHWH RAPHA', THE LORD WILL HEAL

Living for any amount of time on the earth quickly reveals that our world is broken by sin and the consequence of sin: death. "Just as sin came into the world through one man, and death through sin, and so death spread to all men because all sinned" (Rom. 5:12). In YHWH's great mercy, after Adam and Eve sinned in the Garden of Eden, the LORD forbade them and the rest of mankind from access to the Tree of Life, lest they live forever ruled by their sin natures and eternally experience the consequences of their sin (Gen. 3:22-24). Consequently, every human body will eventually wear out. Even those who have become new in Christ experience great suffering on the earth. Christians wage war with the spiritual forces of evil, their own sinful flesh, and experience mourning, crying, and pain. As we consider the fallen state of our world, we find our desperate need for the LORD's healing and restoration. Do you find within your heart a deep longing for the healing of the LORD?

Over the next two weeks, we will be taking a deep look at YHWH Rapha'. In Exodus 15, the LORD ascribes to His name, "Will Heal." Remember that when we read "LORD" in the Bible, it is the Hebrew word "YHWH," which is the personal name for God. To attach any description to His name is to describe an aspect of the nature and character of God. The Hebrew word, "Rapha'" is used 67 times throughout the Old Testament. It has a wide range of uses. "Rapha'" is used for both figurative and literal healings, healings by both God and man, and different types of healing (internal and external). Although Abraham ascribed to the LORD the name Provider when he said "YHWH Jireh," The LORD names Himself Healer. This gives added weight to the name, YHWH Rapha': The LORD Will Heal. Does this mean that it is always God's will to heal His people on this side of Heaven? Does the LORD's name imply that since He Will Heal that He also never inflicts suffering? If the LORD Will Heal is His name, does God allow suffering to accomplish His good purposes?

As we consider these questions, we will be studying the LORD's healing power provided for our spiritual sickness, emotional wounds, and physical ailments. Our rejection or acceptance of God's healing provided in Jesus for our spiritual sickness has the largest consequence. When we look at Jesus' healing for our emotional pain, we find that He is by nature the restorer of our souls and the healer of our hearts. We will also behold Jesus' miraculous healing power yet learn to submit to His plan to bring about fruit in our lives and glory to His great name. It is important to recognize that there will be suffering and pain in every person's life, yet the LORD Will Heal will never cease to manifest His character as Healer. Hardship on earth serves as a reminder that there will be complete healing in Heaven for all of those whose names are found written in the Lamb's Book of Life. As the story of history unfolds, everything is pointing to the realization of perfect healing in Heaven for those who belong to Christ. "He will wipe away every tear from their eyes, and death shall be no more, neither shall there be mourning, nor crying, nor pain anymore …" (Rev. 21:4). The mourning involved in living life on earth is a vapor (Jam. 4:14), yet complete healing in Heaven is for all eternity because YHWH is Our Healer. Throughout this study of the LORD's nature as healer, ask God for His wisdom and help in answering tough questions related to His character as YHWH Rapha'.

MONDAY AND TUESDAY (DAY 1 AND 2): BUILDING CONTEXT

Over the next two days, you will be diving into Scripture that builds the necessary context for the use of YHWH Rapha' in Exodus 15. Leading up to the main YHWH Rapha' text, the Israelites experienced unbearable burdens, pains, afflictions, and deaths on their journey to spiritual healing and deliverance. When the Israelites came to Egypt to live in the land of Goshen, they came in peace and experienced peace. Unfortunately, Egypt quickly became known to them as a place of oppression and slavery. A new king in Egypt arose who became alarmed about the vast number of Israelites. Pharaoh feared that they would become strong enough to overtake the Egyptians because regardless of the heavy burdens and oppression in which they were afflicted, God made the Israelites fruitful, and they multiplied in the land of their suffering. Exodus 1:13-14 says that the Egyptians "ruthlessly made the people of Israel work as slaves and made their lives bitter with hard service." When Pharaoh's efforts to decrease the population failed, Pharaoh commanded that every Hebrew son born be cast into the Nile. Were the Israelites experiencing healing as their baby boys were dying? In those moments, were they experiencing YHWH Rapha'? Did they believe in the LORD as the one that heals? The Israelites probably would not have felt as though God was healer in those moments, but circumstances do not change who God is, nor His nature.

In His mercy, God raised up a deliverer named Moses. The LORD tasked Moses with delivering His message to Pharaoh commanding the release of the children of Israel from Egypt. Throughout Israel's history recorded in the book of Exodus, we find that God is "working all things for the good of those who love Him and are called according to His purposes" (Rom. 8:28) in the midst of terrible suffering. We discover that God does not abandon His people in the midst of their affliction. The pain He allows, He is faithful to use for His mighty purposes and His name's sake. As you take a deep look at the context leading up to the LORD ascribing to His name the word "rapha'," look for examples and glimpses of His nature throughout the Israelites' experiences. Then, consider how YHWH Rapha' has revealed His nature to you throughout your life.

READ EXODUS 6:1-13.
What covenant did God make in the past?

What made God remember His covenant with the nation of Israel?

How do you think the Israelites were affected physically, emotionally, and spiritually by their afflictions in Egypt?

What promise did God make regarding the Israelites' enslavement in Egypt?

When Moses spoke the LORD's promise to the Israelites, what was their response? Why do you think that they responded this way?

Do you see evidence of YHWH Rapha' (spiritually, emotionally, or physically)? If so, explain.

SKIM THROUGH EXODUS 7-12.
Record the ten plagues that God sent upon Egypt in order to bring about their release from slavery.

Note: Moses, and ultimately God, led the Israelites out of Egypt. God led the people around by way of the wilderness toward the Red Sea using a pillar of fire to give them light at night and a pillar of cloud by day to lead them along their way.

READ EXODUS 14.
After releasing the Israelites from slavery, Pharaoh decided to pursue them with chariots and his army. What are the reasons provided in scripture for Pharaoh's mind and heart change?

How did the Israelites respond to the pursuit of the Egyptians? Have you ever experienced something that caused you to respond similarly? Explain.

In response to their fear, what did
Moses say to the Israelites?

In light of Psalm 46:10 and Exodus 14:13-14, describe
how God wants His followers to respond to trials?

According to verses 17-18, for whose glory
is the LORD concerned? What reason does
the LORD give for receiving the glory over
Pharaoh and Pharaoh's chariots and horses?

Focusing on verse 31, in what ways do you think that
Israel grew spiritually? (See also, Proverbs 9:10.)

READ EXODUS 15:11-13.

How did the people of Israel respond to God's great power?

In these passages, we witness God exercising both judgment and mercy. In His Sovereignty, He chose for many Egyptians to be drowned in the Red Sea. The reason given for this incredible act of judgment can be found in Exodus 14:4. His actions were for His glory that the Egyptians might "know that I am the LORD." Although the LORD brought down His righteous judgment upon the Egyptians, it was an act of healing. Healing came to the Egyptians that were not destroyed in the Red Sea as they came to the understanding that the God of the Israelites is the LORD of all. Healing came to the Israelites as the LORD responded to their feelings of abandonment and great affliction in Egypt as He rescued and delivered them with great power. The people of Israel certainly didn't deserve to be delivered from their enemies due to their lack of faith and faint hearts, but God displayed His glory on their behalf in order to display His power so that "the people feared the LORD, and they believed in the LORD" (Exod. 14:31). Likewise, the Egyptians did not deserve for the LORD to show them His truth: "I am the LORD" (Exod. 14:4).

It can be concluded that the LORD is deeply concerned with His own glory because He is the only one who can save. Displays of His glory revealed Himself as the one, true God so that sinful humans might come to repentance and faith in Him. The LORD Our Healer chooses to reveal His glory due to His mercy because it is only in relationship with Him that men and women have hope for true, lasting healing. In studying the passages leading up to Exodus 15, we come to understand that trials, deliverance from trials, acts of judgment, acts of mercy, death, and healings are all for His glory. All of these events are woven together by the loving, sovereign LORD so that people might know Him and believe in Him. He decides what will accomplish the most healing for His glory and the fame of His great name — YHWH Rapha'. Whatever means He chooses to use to bring healing can be trusted because it is His infinite character to act in ways that produce the most healing. Do you trust the LORD Our Healer's work in your life as you face pain and unbearable difficulties? Rest in Him today.

WEDNESDAY AND THURSDAY (DAY 3 AND 4): YHWH RAPHA'

After their experience at the Red Sea, the Israelites should have felt protected and cared for because they had just beheld the power and greatness of God on their behalf as He delivered them out of slavery. The context leading up to use of YHWH Rapha' is shocking because the Israelites quickly abandoned their faith in the might of God and begin to fear greatly for their lives because they lacked water in the wilderness. Sometimes, unpleasant circumstances expose our lack of faith in YHWH as Healer. In the Israelites' case, they grumbled against their Healer in light of a life-threatening circumstance — lack of water. Although the LORD would heal their weary bodies by providing them with water, the true sickness within the Israelites lied within their hearts — they doubted YHWH Rapha'. They lacked faith, and without faith it is impossible to please God (Heb. 11:6).

In His mercy, the LORD provided His people with a lesson regarding His character as the Healer of their lives as a means of increasing their faith in Himself — YHWH Rapha'. The Israelites had witnessed the Lord inflict upon the Egyptians terrifying plagues and even death due to their hardness of heart, yet the LORD choose to give the hard-hearted Israelites an understanding of Himself as Healer. The LORD Will Heal explained to His people that because His character is to bring healing, they can trust that obedience to His commands will result in healing rather than the diseases that inflicted the Egyptians in their disobedience (Exod. 15:26). As you study, ask the LORD Will Heal to reveal Himself to you through His Word. Allow Him to remind you that His commands are not burdensome (1 John 5:3); rather, His commands are given to His people as a gift. His commands magnify His nature as YHWH Rapha'.

READ EXODUS 15:22-26.
What issues were the Israelites
and their livestock facing?

Describe what you think the Israelites
might have been saying and thinking.

Who did the Israelites grumble against?
Do you think that their grumblings were
warranted? Explain your reasoning.

READ 1 THESSALONIANS 5:16-18.
What areas in your life are you quick to grumble
against others and, ultimately, God Almighty?

How could you apply 1 Thessalonians 5:16-18 to your complaining and grumbling?

What indicators do you see in Scripture
that Moses was a good leader?

In what ways have you experienced
God's restoring/healing power?

READ EXODUS 15:22-26.
What miracle did the LORD do?

READ 2 CORINTHIANS 5:17.
What spiritual parallel can be made between
God turning the bitter water to sweet water
and the work God does within a believer?

What two things did the LORD do in verse 25?

In your own words, what did the LORD command in verse 26?

Moses obeyed the command of the LORD to throw the log into the water. Then, the bitter waters were made sweet. How does this event illustrate God's command and promise in verse 26?

What name does the LORD ascribe to Himself?

What is significant about His name?

A person can survive for roughly three days without water; therefore, it is safe to assume that the Israelites and their livestock were experiencing great distress after walking in the wilderness without water for three days. Their situation was an enormous problem; therefore, they were no-doubt relieved to find a body of water — until they discovered that the water was unhealthy to drink. This was their breaking point as they surrendered their trust in God and grumbled against the deliverer, Moses, that

God had provided. YHWH indicated in verse 25 that he "tested them" in reference to the Israelites. In James 1:2-4, we are commanded to "count it all joy ... when we meet trials ..." because "the testing of your faith produces steadfastness." YHWH Rapha' is not a vengeful God that enjoys watching His people suffer from extreme thirst. He is concerned with producing within His people the steadfastness that is necessary to stay faithful to YHWH until one's dying day. Faith-tests teach great lessons and build within one's heart what is needed. Unfortunately, the faith-test of great thirst was failed by the Israelites as they accused God of sinning against them through their haughty complaints.

Moses, on the other hand, passed the test as He cried out to God for help and responded to His command in obedience. It is the type of response to difficulty that Moses displayed that resulted in healing. Moses took the Israelites' complaints and turned them into pleas to God for His intervention. God faithfully showed Moses a log to throw into the water, and Moses obeyed the command of God, resulting in the water's healing. It was not the log that healed the waters, but God's power in response to Moses' obedience. The Lord promised that listening to His voice, obeying His commands, and keeping His statutes as Moses had modeled would protect the Israelites from the diseases that He inflicted upon the Egyptians. Obedience to YHWH brings healing. This healing is not always physical. We would be wrong to think of our obedience to God as a means of manipulating the LORD into doing our bidding. We obey the LORD because we love Him (John 14:15), want to bring Him glory, and trust that His commands, when followed, keep us in His blessing. His commands are gifts to us designed for our good. Our obedience to the LORD will never be perfect on this side of Heaven due to the sinfulness of our flesh, but a life committed to faith and repentance is a life that brings the ultimate healing of eternal life in Heaven. His commands lead to eternal life (John 12:50).

It was after the Israelites drank from the miraculously fresh water that YHWH ascribed to His personal and holy name the word "Rapha'," which means "will heal." The LORD desired that His people relate Himself to the lifesaving, healed waters of which they drank. YHWH was faithful to teach His people that healing would only characterize their lives if they remained committed to the Healer, as shown by their continued obedience to His statutes.

Another misconception that must be addressed in light of this passage is that disobedience is always the cause of one's sickness and/or hardship. When Jesus and His disciples encountered a man that had been blind since birth, the disciples assumed that either the blind man or his parents' sins had resulted in the man's blindness. Jesus addressed this misconception by stating: "It was not that this man sinned, or his parents, but that the works of God might be displayed in him" (John 9:3). Sometimes, men and women of God experience physical suffering so that the works of God might be displayed.

The enemy is always at work tempting us to become bitter toward YHWH. He uses tribulation and painful situations to sow seeds of doubt about the LORD's character as Healer. Satan used this strategy with the Israelites, and he will continue to use this strategy leading up to the end of the age. As war, famine, earthquakes, tribulation, persecution, betrayal, false prophets, and lawlessness increase, "the love of many will grow cold," but "the one who endures to the end will be saved" (Matt. 24:7-13). As you face difficulties, cling to your Healer; do not allow your love for YHWH to grow cold and endure the trials with faith in the LORD Will Heal. Ask God to reveal Himself as the one who demands obedience and greatly rewards those who heed His commands. Remember, you will be surrounded by many who fail faith tests in difficult circumstances; therefore, ask the LORD Will Heal to help you run to Him when you have reached your breaking point.

FRIDAY (DAY 5):
REFLECTION

As you reflect upon the past week of Bible study, prayerfully and honestly answer the following questions.

> Throughout this week of study, what points refined your thinking about the LORD?

How has the Holy Spirit convicted you throughout this past week during your study of God's Word?

Write a prayer to YHWH Rapha' asking for His forgiveness. "If we confess our sins, he is faithful and just to forgive us our sins and to cleanse us from all unrighteousness" (1 John 1:9).

MONDAY AND TUESDAY (DAY 6 AND 7): HEALING FROM SIN SICKNESS AND EMOTIONAL PAIN

"Bless the LORD, O my soul, and forget not all his benefits, who forgives all your iniquity, who heals all your diseases, who redeems your life from the pit, who crowns you with steadfast love and mercy, who satisfies you with good so that your youth is renewed like the eagle's" (Ps. 103:2-5). In these verses, the healing from all diseases can refer to physical healing. In our fallen, fleshly shells, we experience many physical afflictions which cause us to long for physical healing. These afflictions sometimes follow us to the grave, but certainly not into eternity if we are in Christ. "Heals all your diseases" is sandwiched between two phrases that refer to Jesus' healing of our sin sickness: "forgives all your iniquity" and "redeems your life from the pit." Upon looking at the phrase "heals all of your diseases" in context, we can conclude that the healing from diseases spoken of in this verse could also indicate healing from the disease of depravity. Jesus Christ alone can save us from being dead in our sins, lost, and without hope. The deadliest disease we face is our sin; therefore, humbly ask Jesus to convict you of sin and sanctify your heart as you study His Word.

In addition to sin sickness, many of our emotional hurts come from situations that are completely out of our control and beyond our understanding. For example, Job was a righteous man who was afflicted by Satan according to the LORD's will. The LORD Will Heal allowed these trials in Job's life, was faithful to Job during his suffering, and restored and healed him so that his grief ended. In those moments, we learn to trust completely in the sovereignty and goodness of God. Job faithfully states, "For He inflicts pain, and gives relief; He wounds, and His hands also heal (Rapha')" (Job 5:18). YHWH Rapha' is truly wiser than us and sees the end from the beginning. His plan is always to work circumstances for the good of those who love Him and are called according to His purposes (Rom. 8:28). He defines that "good" as the redeemed "being conformed into the image of His Son" (Rom. 8:29). Every circumstance is an opportunity to grow in Christlikeness. Pain and wounds are weaved into God's good plan as sanctifying tools that expose and uproot sin in our lives, strengthen our faith and trust in YHWH, and draw us closer to the person of Christ. Every time a believer chooses to bring glory to YHWH by remaining steadfast in the midst of suffering, they are storing up eternal reward in heaven: the crown of life (Jam. 1:12), repayment for good deeds (Matt. 16:27), His joy (Matt. 25:21), and more. The LORD's good purposes in suffering and the saints' eternal rewards for patient endurance reflect the character of YHWH Rapha'.

Some of our emotional pain is due to our own personal sin and the sins committed against us. Our thoughts, attitudes, feelings, and emotions are affected deeply by sin. King David committed adultery with Bathsheba, the wife of Uriah. Then, through a strategic order to have Uriah moved to the front lines, he murdered Uriah. The consequence for David's sin was excruciating, but God did not leave David in his misery and faithfully proved His constant character as YHWH Rapha', despite David's brutality. As we look at the life of Job, we relate on some degree to the emotional pain associated with living a righteous life on the earth in which "the devil prowls around like a roaring lion, seeking someone to devour" (1 Pet. 5:8). We too are in desperate need of the LORD's healing and protection from the evil one and his schemes. As we look at the life of David, we find that we too suffer the consequences of our sins. As you study the LORD's character as Healer, ask the LORD Will Heal to reveal His nature to you — even in the midst of Job and David's broken-heartedness. Ask the LORD to help you cling to His healing nature in the midst of your personal struggles.

READ EPHESIANS 2:1-3.
Describe a person before they come
to saving faith in Jesus Christ.

What parallels can be made between
sin and sickness/disease?

READ ISAIAH 53:5-6 ALONGSIDE 1 PETER 2:24-25.
Due to Jesus' wounds, crushing, and stripes on the
cross, in what ways do Christians experience healing?

What spiritual sickness did you experience
in your life prior to your salvation?

READ EPHESIANS 2:4-10.
In what ways do we experience spiritual healing?

How does spiritual healing affect
our position with God?

Who is responsible for our salvation
and healing? Explain.

How have you experienced spiritual
healing in your life?

READ JOB 1:13-22.
Describe the afflictions and losses of Job. How do
you think he felt emotionally after such news?

How did Job respond to the events that undoubtedly broke his heart? (See also, Job 3:11, Job 3:26, Job 10:1, Job 30:15-17.)

In what ways have you been emotionally hurt? Describe your response. Does your response show faith in YHWH Rapha'? If not, in what ways do you believe that God is leading you to change?

READ JOB 42:10 AND 12.
What evidence of YHWH Rapha' do you find in the restoration of Job's fortunes?

READ 2 SAMUEL 12:15-23.
How would you describe the condition of David's soul (mind, will, and emotions) while his child was sick? Consider also Psalm 41:4: "As for me, I said, 'O LORD, be gracious to me; Heal my soul, for I have sinned against You.'"

What did David do after he learned that his child had died?

What evidence do you find of David's repentance in this passage?

In what ways have you experienced God's healing from sin that caused you heartache?

READ JAMES 5:16.
If you are living in bondage to sin, how might you apply this verse to your life?

Before a true salvation experience, human beings are spiritually dead. Completely dead in trespasses and by nature objects of wrath — men and women alike have absolutely nothing to offer God except sin and rebellion. In Isaiah 53:5-6, we read that the crushing of Jesus makes peace possible between the LORD and those that come to saving faith in Christ. In 1 Peter 2:24, we find that Jesus bore our sins in His body so that we could experience healing — spiritual healing. The most profound healing that we experience, only through Christ, is the putting off of our old self and becoming a new creation in Christ. This healing is a free gift from YHWH Rapha' made possible through Jesus' atoning sacrifice on the cross.

Despite becoming a new creation in Christ, Christians are not exempt from emotional wounds. Due to our sin, effects of living in a fallen world, and being surrounded by other sinful humans, emotional hurt is a part of life. Sometimes our pain is so overwhelming that we relate to Jesus' lament in the Garden of Gethsemane as He prepared to suffer and die: "My soul is consumed with sorrow to the point of death" (Matt. 26:38). No one is exempt from emotional pain while on earth. Some emotional hurts are self-inflicted due to sin. Some are inflicted by the sins of others and require our forgiveness. Some, like death, are a part of living in a fallen world that is sin-stricken. Amid all emotional wounds, the LORD Will Heal His people as they cry out to Him. He heals the brokenhearted and binds up their wounds (Ps. 147:3).

Today, praise the LORD Will Heal for making you alive in Himself through His chastisement on the cross. When emotional burdens weigh heavy on your heart, turn to YHWH Rapha' saying, though "my flesh and my heart may fail … God is the strength of my heart and my portion forever" (Ps. 73:26). After hearing of the death of his child, David chose to enter into the house of the LORD and worshipped YHWH. After Job heard of the destruction of his children and property, he mourned, fell to the ground, and worshipped (Job 1:20). Worship YHWH today. Whatever your emotional burden might be, bless the name of YHWH Rapha'. Jesus, YHWH in the flesh, binds up the brokenhearted, gives His people gladness instead of mourning, and grants them the ability to praise instead of abandoning them to a faint spirit (Isa. 61:1,3). Draw near to YHWH Rapha'; He will not forsake you to despair.

WEDNESDAY AND THURSDAY (DAY 8 AND 9): HEALING FROM EMOTIONAL PAIN CAUSED BY OTHERS AND PHYSICAL WOUNDS

Throughout the next two days, we will study Scripture surrounding the sovereign time-table of YHWH Rapha' in regard to physical healing and the response that He commands whenever we are emotionally wronged by another. YHWH Rapha', the LORD Will Heal, is the author of healing. Does this mean that the LORD always decides to heal physical ailments on this side of Heaven? Although the LORD is able to completely heal, we as creation must never insist or presume that He must heal our wounds. In regard to physical healing, we can stand on the promise of complete restoration of our fleshly bodies anew at the return of Christ or whenever we enter into our Heavenly home. We are called to believe in the LORD Will Heal and in His healing power today, but also submit to His sovereignty as to when our physical healing occurs. Regardless, we can pray alongside the prophet Jeremiah "Heal me, O LORD, and I will be healed; save me and I will be saved, for You are my praise" (Jer. 17:14). We can rest assured, that if the LORD Will Heal inflicts or allows wounding, hurts, or pain it is for the purpose of bringing about inner healing. There is "a time to kill and a time to heal; a time to tear down and a time to build up" (Eccles. 3:3). As you study, ask God to help you submit to His sovereignty on the timing for your physical healing.

In regard to emotional wounds and pain, when we are wronged by others, self-righteousness is a temptation. Often, in light of an offense, our minds become consumed with the wrong inflicted upon us instead of our own imperfections and offenses against God. Jesus does not belittle or discount our hurts at the hands of others, but He does command us to respond to offenses with humility and forgiveness. When we choose to set our minds on the underserved forgiveness of God, He molds our hearts to love our enemies and pray for those that hurt us. Are you holding on to unforgiveness? Today, ask God to reveal areas of unforgiveness in your heart and repent. Ask God for grace to respond to others in a way that is worthy of Him.

READ MATTHEW 5:43-48.
How does Jesus teach us to respond to the hurts, persecution, and evil done against us?

How does the way we respond to the hurts from others reflect YHWH Rapha's character?

READ COLOSSIANS 3:12-14.
How does God expect us to respond to those that sin against us?

Forgiveness of others is a command. What reason is given for this command?

READ MATTHEW 6:14-15.
Why might someone who refuses to forgive a fellow sinner not experience the forgiveness of God?

READ MATTHEW 9:18-26.
What similarities are there between the two healings? What are the differences?

How does the following Psalm relate to Matthew 9:18-26? "O LORD my God, I cried to You for help, and You healed me (Rapha')" Psalm 30:2.

How might the healings of the little girl and the woman with the issue of blood have brought about spiritual healing in the lives of those involved in the events that took place?

READ 2 CORINTHIANS 12:7-10.
What was Paul experiencing?

What did he ask of God?

How did God answer?

Have you ever asked God for the removal of a thorn? What was His answer to you? How can you apply this passage to your situation?

YHWH Rapha' commands that we forgive others. How is this possible? Why is this required? When one comes to Christ, they come with an abundance of sin against the Holy, Holy, Holy LORD God Almighty. If one is in Christ, the Holy Spirit has revealed to them their sin and need for a Savior. To withhold forgiveness from someone is to scoff at the great offenses we have committed against the LORD and to say with our actions that a person's offense against us is greater and more important than all of our past, present, and future offenses against the LORD. A second thought to consider on this topic is that in commanding forgiveness, Jesus remains YHWH Rapha'. Forgiveness produces healing. When we forgive others out of obedience to the LORD, He heals our hearts. When we bless and pray for those who have wronged us, He does a miracle within us by changing our hearts to align with His. Ask God today to help you forgive your offender, no matter the offense, so that you can reflect His character. Truly, nothing is impossible with God.

It is encouraging to know that YHWH Rapha' is the One who is sovereign. The LORD attaches "Will Heal" to His divine name. The implication of His name is that He will do and/or allow what produces the healing that we need. What if in divinely choosing to temporarily leave one with a physical ailment it produces abundant and eternal spiritual healing in the lives of many? When we do not understand His timing or His reasons for withholding miraculous healing power, we can choose to trust in His goodness as the Healer. Consider the great physical suffering of Jesus that resulted in our redemption. We can and should pray alongside Jesus, "Father, if you are willing, remove this cup from me. Nevertheless, not my will, but yours, be done" (Luke 22:42). We can stand on the truth that the suffering that YHWH Rapha' plans in our lives will not be wasted. There is purpose in pain. Healing is on the horizon. YHWH Rapha' can be trusted.

FRIDAY (DAY 10): REFLECTION

Regarding spiritual healing, Jesus has won our victory and paid the price for those He calls to be saved and makes new creations in Christ. In regard to emotional healing, a person in Christ can experience the Comforter, rest for their souls, and joy for their sorrow. When we consider physical healing, God is able and powerful to perform miraculous healings today according to His Will. Take time to reflect upon the LORD Will Heal's work in your life.

How have you experienced the LORD Will Heal's spiritual, emotional, and physical healing power?

Write a prayer to Jesus. Begin by thanking Him for the many blessings and gifts in your life. Then, humbly ask God for the emotional, spiritual, or physical healing needed in your life. Consider ending your prayer using the words of Jesus, "Father, if you are willing, remove this cup from me. Nevertheless, not my will, but yours, be done" (Luke 22:42).

LESSON 3: YHWH NISSI, THE LORD IS MY BANNER

Throughout the next two weeks, we will focus on another name ascribed to the LORD: YHWH Nissi. This compound name of the LORD is only found in Exodus 17:15. As stated in previous weeks, YHWH is the personal name for God which comes from the Hebrew word, "YHWH." "YHWH" is written in English as "LORD." The word, "nissi," is attached to God's holy, personal name; therefore, "nissi" describes one of God's divine attributes and explains His unchanging character. There are far less words in the Hebrew language; therefore, the word "nissi" has many translations in English. The uses of "nissi" throughout the Bible sometimes refers to banners, symbols, or signs. Sometimes, "nissi" is used to describe something that represents a standard or rallying point for a group of people. By attaching it to the LORD's name, "nissi" signifies that the LORD is the symbol to rally around and the standard to uphold.

"Nissi" was ascribed to the LORD by Moses when he built and named an altar after the Israelites miraculously defeated the Amalekites. All odds seemed to be stacked against the Israelites as they entered into battle against the skilled, pagan warriors. The Israelites were ex-slaves who were historically from a line of shepherds (i.e., not warriors), and they traveled with women, children, and possessions. Through the Israelites' amazing defeat of the Amalekites, The LORD Is My Banner revealed Himself as the One worth identifying with, holding high, and placing all hope and trust in for every battle — both physical and spiritual. He was the One in which they were to proudly rally around and raise above themselves.

In further understanding YHWH Nissi, it is helpful to consider where we use banners in the present day. When we identify with certain schools, teams, states, and countries by raising up banners and flags in their honor, we proudly wave their banners saying, "I belong to this ..." The banners in our lives are the things that we rally around and claim as our identity. People uphold money, power, success, fame, family members, certain friends, positions, and others as banners in their lives. Anytime we find our identity and rally around someone or something that isn't God in our time of need, we are guilty of idolatry. Throughout this study, ask The LORD Is My Banner to show you banners in your life that are idolatrous and taking the place that rightfully belongs to YHWH Nissi. Ask the LORD to give you courage to rally around Him and represent Him.

MONDAY AND TUESDAY (DAY 1 AND 2): BUILDING CONTEXT

Throughout the next two days, we will be studying the context leading up to a mighty victory the Israelites won against their enemies, the Amalekites. After learning about The LORD Will Heal, the LORD had a new lesson for His people. The only use of YHWH Nissi in the Bible lands two chapters after the use of YHWH Rapha' in Exodus 15. Roughly a month and a half after their Exodus from Egypt, the Israelites began to long for the food that they ate while enslaved in Egypt. Their complaints and lack of faith were answered lovingly and mercifully by YHWH Jireh as He provided morning bread and evening meat. The LORD gave the Israelites specific gathering instructions that were disobeyed. The Israelites' disobedience revealed their lack of faith in the same God that parted the Red Sea and performed many miracles so that they might know that He is the LORD God. Clearly, they were not proudly waving the LORD as their banner as they disobeyed and complained.

In Exodus 17, the Israelites quarreled against Moses and tested the LORD due to their thirst. This marks the third time that the Israelites did not trust in the LORD to provide for their basic needs. Despite the LORD's power displays, Israel still doubted that the LORD was among them. They did not yet uphold the LORD as their banner. They did not know Him as their rallying point in the midst of affliction. As you study the Scripture between the use of YHWH Rapha' and YHWH Nissi, ask The LORD Is My Banner to highlight to you what particular actions displayed by the Israelites revealed that they had not come to know and uphold God as the banner of their lives. Remember, our disobedience and complaints against the LORD prove whether or not we truly recognize the LORD as YHWH Nissi. Who do you run to in affliction? Who do you raise above yourself and identify with in your suffering? Ask the LORD to refine you like gold through the study of His Word.

READ EXODUS 16:1-3.
Who grumbled against Moses and Aaron?

What was their complaint?

READ EXODUS 16:4-12?
Jesus declares that He is "the bread that came down from Heaven" (John 6:41). What parallels do you find between the bread provided for the Israelites and Jesus Christ?

What was the purpose of the LORD's specific gathering directions?

How does the LORD respond to the grumblings against Himself?

What do you glean about the LORD's character through His response?

READ EXODUS 16:13-21.
Why do you think the Israelites chose not to listen to Moses (and God) and kept part of the manna until the next day?

What was the consequence for storing manna?

What correlation can be made between the Israelites' disobedience and worms (some translations use "maggots"), and our disobedience and the consequences for our own sin?

READ EXODUS 16:22-36.

What is the contrast between the manna kept on the weekdays versus manna kept for the Sabbath day? What does this show us about God?

Some Israelites went out to gather manna on the Sabbath. What was Moses' response?

READ EXODUS 17:1-7.

In what ways did the people of Israel test the LORD in this passage?

How did the LORD respond to His people?

READ PSALM 95:8-9.

What was the condition of the Israelites' hearts?

In this passage, we beheld hard-hearted Israelites rallying their affection and attention around Egypt's meat pots and abundant bread as they complained against the LORD regarding their current hungry state in the wilderness. We uncovered that the Israelites trusted in the provided manna by storing up more than they were commanded to by God. Their hoarding revealed that they cared more about securing their own needs than walking in obedience to the One who delivered them out of slavery in Egypt. Full of pride, the Israelites' actions proved that they were rallying around themselves to meet to their own needs. They sought to control their situation and trusted in their finite knowledge. The Israelites were holding up many banners, but YHWH was not one of them. Any banner that is upheld in the stead of YHWH is an idol.

Pharaoh and the Egyptians were previously described as hard-hearted in Exodus 14:8. In the passages of Scripture studied throughout the past two days, the Israelites demonstrated that their hearts were also hard. Their actions revealed that they still did not understand YHWH. They certainly had not come to know Him as The LORD Is My Banner, yet the LORD mercifully and patiently taught them that He is sustainer, provider, healer and the only one worth rallying around for His Name's sake. After their experiences in Egypt and the wilderness, the LORD should have been the banner that they held high. Instead, the Israelites tested the LORD with questions and complaints. They asked, "Is the LORD among us or not" (Exod. 17:7)? Such a question was like asking, "Is the LORD even real? Does He even care about us?" Even worse, such questioning took place after multiple miracles in which the LORD displayed His glory. He had delivered the Israelites from slavery in Egypt, parted the Red Sea to provide safe passage, turned bitter waters into sweet waters, and rained down manna from Heaven in the morning, and provided quail in the evening. How could they still question whether the LORD was among them or not?

But do we not do the same thing today? Forgetting the faithfulness of God, we are prone to call into question His very character when our circumstances do not meet our expectations. "God, are you listening? God, do you even love me? Are you really good?" Such questioning reveals that we have forgotten that we are not entitled to anything by the God of the universe. The Set-Apart, Holy One is not like us in any way, and His ways are vastly beyond our ways (Is. 55:8-9). YHWH Nissi had proved His love, care, and presence among the Israelites just as He proved His love for us by dying for us while we were still dead in our sins (Rom. 5:8). Instead of responding to the Israelites' wicked grumblings with wrath, He decided to let Israel "see the glory of the LORD" (Exod. 16:7). Everything YHWH does is for His glory and displays His character perfectly. Although in our finite understanding of an infinite God, we might interpret God's acts for His glory as selfish, this would be a wrong interpretation. The LORD's concern with His glory is overwhelmingly loving because His glory displays Himself — the only One by which men and women find life.

In anticipation of Wednesday and Thursday's Bible Study regarding the only use of YHWH Nissi in the Bible, remember that instead of abandoning the Israelites in their weakness and snuffing out their small flames of belief, YHWH Nissi had a plan. In response to the Israelites hard hearts, the LORD planned to reveal Himself as victorious! He was going to give them a powerful lesson in His identity as The LORD Is My Banner.

WEDNESDAY AND THURSDAY (DAY 3 AND 4): THE LORD IS MY BANNER

Approaching the battle with the Amalekites, the Israelites were not a band of warriors that were skilled and ready for battle; rather, they were ex-slaves historically from a line of shepherds that had been wandering in the wilderness. No doubt, they were tired and ill-equipped for battle. Nonetheless, a powerful enemy approached to attack them while they camped at Rephidim. The odds were impossible for the Israelites, and both the Amalekites and Israelites knew it. Regardless of the impossible odds, Moses commanded Joshua to lead the Israelites into battle against the Amalekites as He raised the staff of God above Himself as the battle raged.

Through the ups and downs within the great, day-long battle against the Amalekites, the Israelites were being taught a valuable lesson: Numbers, battle-skills, and strategy have little to do with victory. This particular battle depended upon Moses' surrender to the character of the LORD Is My Banner, evidenced through his raised staff and hands. The staff that Moses raised was his shepherd staff that he used as he shepherded his father-in-law's flocks prior to being called by God to lead the Israelites out of slavery. The staff of a shepherd was primarily used to lead the flock and to defend against predators that sought to harm the sheep. With its use in mind, it's no wonder God chose this staff to be a symbol of His leadership, Sovereignty, and control over everyone and His defense against anyone who sought to harm His people. This staff was used by YHWH to carry out might acts of protection on behalf of the Israelites leading up to the battle with the Amalekites. The staff did not have power, it was simply a symbol and chosen instrument to carry out YHWH's leadership and defense of His people.

In the past, God had told Moses "Take up your staff and do …" In this passage, it seems to be Moses' plan to raise up the staff. As Moses raises up the staff of God, He is making the statement in the midst of affliction: "YHWH, I trust in your leadership. I trust in your defense and protection. You have done mighty things in the past, and I am raising you up as our hope in affliction." Moses meant to indicate by using the staff, that he looked to God alone for victory, and did not raise up the power and might of humans as his banner while going into battle. As you face battles, where do you find your strength? Who do you rally around and raise above yourself as your banner? Ask YHWH Nissi to reveal to you the way He wants you to respond to the battles you face. Ask Him to reveal His glory to you so that you might give Him the place as the banner of your life.

READ EXODUS 17:8-16.
Leading up to the battle at Rephidim, what experience had the people of Israel had in warfare?

Using Deuteronomy 25:17-19, what further details are provided regarding how the conflict between Israel and Amalekites began?

What do these verses reveal about the Amalekites? (See also, Deut. 25:17-19.)

Describe the battle plan that Moses communicated with Joshua.

Who created the battle plan?

Throughout this passage, human weakness is revealed. What details of this historical account reveal Moses' weakness?

What details of this historical account reveal Joshua's weakness?

What does the staff likely represent to the Israelites? (See also, Exod. 4:1-5, 7:20, 14:15-16.)

Why do you think that Moses chose to raise the staff of God in His hands?

What correlations can be made between the raised staff and victory and the lowered staff and defeat? How might this these correlations relate to YHWH Nissi?

Why do you think that the LORD judged the Amalekites saying, "I will utterly blot out the memory of Amalekites from under Heaven?" (See also, Deut. 25:17-19.)

After a great, miraculous victory, what lessons do you think Moses and the Israelites learned?

Why do you think Moses ascribed "Is My Banner" to God's personal name?

What banners do you rally around or trust in for your victories?

What practical steps could you take to make the LORD the banner of your life?

READ ISAIAH 43:1-4.

How do these verses relate to the Israelites' battle with the Amalekites?

In what ways do these verses personally encourage you?

Remember the context leading up to this passage: The Israelites were looking back to Egypt, testing God, and speaking blasphemies against YHWH …"Is the LORD even among us?" Instead of abandoning the Israelites in their weakness and snuffing out their smoldering flames of belief, YHWH Nissi carried out His plan to reveal His identity as The LORD Is My Banner to the hard-hearted Israelites through the Israelites' amazing defeat of the Amalekites. He showed Himself to be the One worth identifying with, holding high, and placing all hope and trust in for every battle.

After hearing about the ruthless attack against the rear of the Israelite camp where surely the elderly, mothers with small children, and other weary members of the congregation resided, Moses formed a plan to answer the attack against the LORD's people. Moses commanded Joshua to lead the able men into battle against the Amalekites while he raised the staff of God high above Himself. When Moses lifted up His hands with the staff of God in them, God gave them victory. The staff was a sign of total dependence upon the one who had led and delivered them in the past. Moses was making a statement in raising up the staff of God: "I remember your faithfulness. I remember your promises. I know you're powerful. So I am trusting in you and raising up my banner — YHWH." Moses looked to God for the Israelites' victory.

YHWH also showed the Israelites that whenever they fail to uphold Him as their banner (symbolized by Moses' hands being down), they would face defeat. Just as the Israelites were conquered whenever the staff of God was not raised up, when we don't uphold The LORD Is My Banner as the rallying point in trials, battles, and afflictions — we will lose. Numbers, battle-skills, strategy, human effort, human planning/control, and human heroes have little to do with victory and are worthless banners to uphold in affliction. Any banner that is not YHWH will utterly fail us in the hour of need; therefore, we must eliminate other banners in our lives that take the place of God. Since we, as sinful flesh, are prone to rally around our own strength and wisdom for victory, we must actively place our faith and trust in Jesus Christ as the One who holds all strength and victory. The righteous response to YHWH Nissi is both obedience and surrender to His plan. Whether we uphold the LORD Is My Banner with our lives or not, He will always and forever be the unchanging King of the Universe who is the banner, rallying point, and sign/symbol to identify with and look to in all circumstances — it is His divine identity.

"Nissi" was ascribed to the LORD by Moses after he named the alter he built after the Israelites miraculously defeated the Amalekites. Alters were built as acts of worship and memorials to remember important historical events. Clearly, Moses did not want himself or the people to forget the lessons they learned through the battle about the unchanging character of God — YHWH Nissi. As we study about YHWH Nissi, it is tempting to make His divine character about us as we demand the type of miraculous victory in our circumstances that God accomplished on behalf of the Israelites. Although LORD is able to do whatever we desire, He in no way promises to deliver us out of our fiery trials. His victory doesn't always unfold according to our expectations or timetable. YHWH Nissi certainly could have worked His plan to result in zero Israelite causalities in this great battle against the Amalekites. He had the power to make the Israelites' problems vanish in an instant, but He chose to let the battle play out in order to sanctify them in the truth that He is the banner and the one worth upholding. In the same way, we find ourselves in the midst of trials because YHWH is concerned about greater victories on our behalf than the victory of a long-life, that's pleasant, and free from distress — those victories are much too temporal. YHWH is committed to teaching His people truths about Himself as He works His Sovereign plan in our lives and prepares us for the eternal weight of glory beyond all comparison in Heaven (2 Cor. 4:17).

FRIDAY (DAY 5):
REFLECTION

Consider the passages studied throughout the week as you answer the reflection questions below thoughtfully, honestly, and prayerfully.

What holds you back from proudly waving the LORD over you as your banner?

Find and record a scripture to cling to when you are tempted to wave another banner in the place of the LORD.

In what ways do you relate to the Israelites?

MONDAY AND TUESDAY (DAY 6 AND 7):
CONNECTION TO CHRIST

In Numbers 21:4-9, we will uncover another Old Testament use of the word "nissi." When "nissi" is attached to YHWH in Exodus 17, it is translated as "banner" in English. Whenever "nissi" is used in Numbers 21, it is translated in English as a "pole" on which a bonze snake is hung and lifted up. Nonetheless, it is the same Hebrew word used in both passages. As the Israelites rallied around YHWH Nissi as their banner of victory, the Israelites later rallied around a bronze snake that resulted in their healing. The use of "nissi" within this passage foreshadows Jesus Christ's atonement for sins.

In preparation for studying this passage, there are a few contextual aspects that need to be considered. This event takes place toward the end of Israel's time in the wilderness, and they are very near to the Promised Land. During their wandering in the desert, the Israelites continually tested God. Consistently, the Israelites complained about their food. In the instance we will study today, the Israelites "spoke against God" (Num. 21:5) because they found their food to be worthless. Speaking against God is quite different than crying out to God in need. The latter is often rewarded in Scripture while speaking against God is condemned. To "speak against God" is to accuse Him of wrongdoing — of sinning against them by not providing for their basic needs correctly. Psalm 78:17-18 states that "they sinned still more against him, rebelling against the Most High in the desert. They tested God in their hearts by demanding the food they craved. They spoke against God, saying, can God spread a table in the wilderness?" The level of pride that the Israelites displayed was out of place after witnessing the LORD's awesome power and might. In addition to the plagues sent against the Egyptians and the judgment against the Egyptians at the Red Sea, the Israelites had trembled in the presence of the LORD at Mount Sinai as He descended upon it in fire and caused it to quake greatly (Exod. 19:18) before the LORD gave the Ten Commandments to Moses. YHWH Nissi had continually performed countless glory displays, yet the Israelites "spoke against Him."

As you study, look for comparisons between Jesus' death on the cross and the bronze serpent erected high on a pole. Ask Jesus to reveal to you through the Holy Spirit any offensive way within you so that you can repent and experience His healing as you learn about His identity as YHWH Nissi.

READ NUMBERS 14:20-23.
At this point in Israel's journey, how many times had the Israelites put the LORD to the test and disobeyed Him?

What was the current generation of the Israelites' punishment for consistently putting the LORD to the test?

READ NUMBERS 21:4-9.
What caused the Israelites to become impatient? (See also, Num. 20:14-21.)

Look up a definition of "impatient." The Israelites' impatience was directed at the LORD. What attitudes and thoughts might the Israelites been harboring against their God?

In what ways did the Israelites sin
against God and Moses?

How did YHWH Nissi justly respond to their sin?

How did the Israelites respond to
God's judgment against them?

What did the LORD command Moses and the
Israelites to do in order to experience His healing and
deliverance from the just punishment for their sins?

Have you ever become impatient with YHWH? If so,
how do you think the LORD would have you respond
to situations that tempt you towards impatience?

READ JOHN 3:14-15.
What comparisons can be made between the lifting up of the bronze serpent and the lifting up of Jesus on the cross?

The Israelites' nissi (pole) resulted in them being spared from God's wrath in Numbers 21. Describe how making Jesus the banner of your life (your rallying point) saves you from God's wrath.

Because the Edomites refused the Israelites' safe and peaceful passage through their land, the Israelites had to turn back toward the wilderness and away from Canaan, the Promised Land. This was obviously discouraging since the Israelites had come so close to the Promised Land, but their impatience against YHWH revealed their heart posture before their holy God. They stated with their impatience, "I know better than you, God. My ways are better than your ways and you have wronged and sinned against me by delaying what I want." Their impatience quickly led to "speaking against God" and standing in judgment over YHWH Nissi. In spite of all that the LORD had done on the Israelites' behalf, "they still sinned; despite His wonders, they did not believe" (Ps. 78:32). Their attitudes of ungratefulness toward the One who had provided them with manna, quail, water, and His very presence throughout their time in the wilderness was answered by YHWH Nissi.

God's response to their sin was to pour out justice: "He made their days vanish like a breath, and their years in terror" (Ps. 78:33). Although sending fiery serpents to kill the Israelites in response to their sin might sound extreme to our finite minds, Psalm 78 tells us that "when the LORD killed them, they sought Him; they repented and sought God earnestly. They remembered that God was their rock, the Most High God their redeemer" (vs. 34-35). The justice of God was matched by His unfailing love. In order for the Israelites to be healed and spared from the judgment God had righteously poured out in response to their sin, they raised up a bronze serpent on a pole and rallied around it. They had to look to their "nissi" for healing. Due to their repentance, "He, being compassionate, atoned for their iniquity, and did not destroy them" (Ps. 78:38).

In Exodus 17, we saw a band of Israelites find miraculous victory as they learned to proudly wave their banner, YHWH Nissi, high above themselves in the midst of afflictions and trials. They rallied around Him for victory and learned to uphold Him as they trusted in His leadership and protection. Our devotion to Jesus should be the same during affliction. We are to look to Him for victory because He overcame death, hell, and the grave when He rose from the dead. In Numbers 21, we studied a band of Israelites, dead in their sins and under the fierce wrath of God look to the fiery serpent on the nissi for their salvation. In the same way, we are to look to Jesus as our Savior and only hope for Salvation. He is the only one who can deliver us from the just wrath against our grievous sins against YHWH.

In response to these truths, we are to raise Jesus as the banner of our lives and our rallying point in affliction. Jesus is to be the one that we look to as the sign and symbol of our lives because He brought about our salvation. Jesus is the one we lift high in our lives, no matter the consequence, because He died for us while we were still sinners. Jesus is the one that we make the LORD of our lives and trust in for leadership and protection. Salvation belongs to YHWH Nissi! May we lift Him high! "For God so loved the world, that He gave His only Son, that whoever believes in Him should not perish but have eternal life. For God did not send His Son into the world to condemn the world, but in order that the world might be saved through Him" (John 3:16-17).

WEDNESDAY AND THURSDAY (DAY 8 AND 9): JESUS IS THE VICTOR, BANNER, AND RALLYING POINT

Throughout the next two days of study, we will search for evidence of YHWH Nissi in the life of Paul using select passages from 2 Corinthians. While the Israelites had to go through battles in order to learn that YHWH Nissi was their victory and the One worth rallying around in the face of opposition, Paul endured suffering with a spirit of thankfulness as he experienced God's victorious power in his ministry. Paul suffered intensely as he labored for the Kingdom of God, but Paul was not always a devout follower of Jesus. Before Paul's conversion, his name was Saul and he was guilty of ravaging the church, dragging men and women out of their houses, and committing anyone claiming Jesus as Christ to prison (Acts 8:3). It was due to his persecution of the Church that Paul considered himself "not worthy to be called an apostle" (1 Cor. 15:9). After the LORD radically encountered and redeemed Saul (Acts 9), he immediately began to proclaim that Jesus was the son of God (Acts 9:20) as he increased in strength and confused the Jews by proving that Jesus was the Christ in the synagogues (Acts 9:20, 22).

Almost immediately after Saul's conversion and name change, He began to face suffering for the sake of the Gospel. At one point, Paul was dragged out of the city of Lystra, and stoned to the point in which he was presumed dead. Though Paul was gravely injured, He was so committed to the mission of spreading the Good News, he arose and entered the city and continued boldly preaching the Gospel the very next day. Instead of throwing in the towel or wallowing in self-pity, Paul encouraged the disciples to continue in the faith despite their many tribulations (Acts 14:19-23). This is just one of the many examples in which Paul found His strength in Jesus and pressed for the sake of the Gospel despite the cost. In 2 Corinthians, Paul describes several situations in which outward appearances reflected defeat, but victory belonged to the LORD. Our battles are undoubtedly different, but like the Israelites and Paul, we face opposition as we war against internal forces, our own sinful desires, attacks from demonic spirits, and attacks from other humans that stand in opposition to us and the Kingdom of God. Opposition will come, but all our hope for victory rests in Jesus Christ. "God is our refuge and strength, a very present help in trouble" (Ps. 46:1). As you study the Scriptures, ask YHWH Nissi to reveal ways in which Paul honored Him so that you can be exhorted to endure trials in a God-honoring way. Examine the Scriptures for examples of Christ's victory in the midst of affliction.

READ 2 CORINTHIANS 1:8-10.
In what way was Paul suffering?
(See also, 2 Cor. 4:8, 17.)

How does Paul describe his emotional
state? (See also, 2 Cor. 4:8, 17.)

What reason did Paul give for His suffering?

How has your suffering taught you to rely on God?

In verse 10, Paul states that God had delivered
them and would do so again. How is this an
example of victory in the face of opposition?

How does hoping in Christ and His Word relate to upholding YHWH Nissi?

READ 2 CORINTHIANS 4:8-18.
List the paradoxes Paul gives to describe the Christian life in light of living in their present, evil age?

How do these paradoxes point to YHWH Nissi, the One who yields victory even in adversity?

In verse 14, what specific promises of God does Paul place his trust in while enduring trials?

What is Paul's attitude during battles?

Why are they able to keep from losing heart in the midst of opposition and affliction?

Do you see Paul upholding YHWH Nissi in these verses? Do you see YHWH Nissi bringing about victory in these verses? Explain.

READ 2 CORINTHIANS 11:23-30.
Create a list of Paul's sufferings as a servant of Christ. Circle the ones to which you relate.

In verse 30, what does Paul say that he will boast in?

Why do you think that Paul boasts in weakness? (See also, 1 Cor. 1:27 and 2 Cor. 12:5-10.)

What is the benefit of a Christian's awareness of their own weakness?

How does weakness remind us to uphold YHWH Nissi?

As a football team that wins the championship proudly waves their team's flag high above themselves, so our devotion to Jesus should be in the midst of affliction. In trials, even when afflicted, perplexed, persecuted, struck down, and given over to death, all our hope rests in Jesus as we thankfully acknowledge the spiritual victories that He is accomplishing in our hearts and the hearts of believers around us. Jesus is faithful to accomplish His eternal work through affliction as He uses terrible circumstances to conform His followers into the image of His Son as they look forward to their glorification with Christ in Heaven (Rom. 8:28-30). It is for this reason that the Apostle Paul encourages the church in Corinth by saying, "look not to the things that are seen but to the things that are unseen. For the things that are seen are transient, but the things that are unseen are eternal" (2 Cor. 4:18). It is sinful human nature to place expectations upon God in regard to our lives. When we focus on the transient, our circumstances might appear unfair and overwhelming which often results in a downward spiral of self-pity and resentment against God. Rather, the people of God are to focus on the eternal work that is being accomplished through suffering. We must surrender our version of "our best life," and trust that Jesus has our best interests in His heart.

Instead of Paul dwelling on His negative circumstances, these passages reveal that Paul stood on the promises of God and hoped in Jesus for eternal victory. There are victories far more important than a long life free from pain and suffering. YHWH Nissi allows many trials in the lives of believers for the purpose of producing within us dependence on God for all strength and victory. We should follow the example of Paul when we fight our battles. We are called to uphold YHWH Nissi as we proclaim and hope in His promises of eternal life and resurrection. He is our banner! He is our victory! When the world seems to be crashing down around us, He is our rallying point. Do you rally around YHWH Nissi?

FRIDAY (DAY 10): REFLECTION

Consider the passages studied throughout this week as you answer the reflection questions below. Ask the Holy Spirit to guide you as you reflect.

In what ways has God used your afflictions/battles to bring about spiritual victory in your life?

In what ways can you adopt a more God honoring mindset in the midst of your battles?

Read the following verses: 1 Corinthians 3:11-14, Matthew 5:12, Revelation 22:12, Philippians 3:14, 1 Corinthians 3:8, Luke 6:22-23, and 2 Timothy 4:8. How do these verses encourage you to adopt an eternal/heavenly perspective in the midst of battles on the earth?

LESSON 4: YHWH MEKADDISHKEM, THE LORD OUR SANCTIFIER

Over the next two weeks, we will be studying a description of YHWH in relation to His people. YHWH Mekaddishkem is used in five places in Scripture and three different books of the Bible. Mekaddishkem, which comes from the Hebrew word "qadash," means to sanctify, make holy, or set apart. YHWH Mekaddishkem is translated several ways: The LORD Our Sanctifier, The LORD Who Sanctifies You, or The LORD Who Makes Holy. Throughout the study of YHWH Mekaddishkem, all three translations will be considered as we seek to understand the LORD as our sanctifier. As "Our Sanctifier" is attached to the LORD's personal name by God Himself, He is revealing one of His divine characteristics as His names express His operations and infinite characteristics. In order to sanctify others, YHWH must be the highest level of holy. The holiness of YHWH requires that He has nothing to do with sin. He is too holy to tolerate even the smallest amount of unity with sin. He is completely separated from sin. It is because of His holiness that YHWH sanctifies, sets apart, and makes holy His people. It is only because of His identity as the LORD Our Sanctifier that we have any hope being counted as holy before the "holy holy holy ... Lord God Almighty, who was and is and is to come" (Rev. 4:8).

In short, to be sanctified is to be made holy by God. When one is made holy by God, they are set apart or separated from wickedness. This is nothing short of a miracle because all people are completely dead in their sins (Eph. 2:1), sinful from birth (Jer. 13:23), and by nature children of wrath (Eph. 2:3). Our depraved, sinful nature leaves us powerless to accomplish sanctification. May His name be praised, for He makes holy those who are both undeserving and incapable of making themselves holy. Upon Salvation, a believer is given the status as "sanctified" in position before YHWH, yet their sin nature is still present. While a Christian remains on the earth, YHWH Mekaddishkem does not deny His nature by abandoning His children to depravity. The LORD Who Sanctifies actively disciplines the children He loves (Heb. 12:6) by exposing sinful behavior and equipping His people to live lives free from the slavery of sin due to the inner work of the Holy Spirit. "But now that

[we] have been set free from sin and have become slaves to God, the fruit [we] reap leads to holiness, and the outcome is eternal life" (Rom. 6:22).

Another noteworthy aspect of YHWH's nature as Mekaddishkem is that He ties His name to His Sabbath commands for His people. Due to His character, He is fully committed to making His people holy. One way He accomplishes His sanctifying work is by requiring Sabbath Day observance. Sabbath day observance is a sign between people and YHWH that He is the LORD Who Makes Holy. By setting apart one day out of the week for worship, focus, and commitment to YHWH, a person is indicating that they are set apart by the only One able to set apart and make holy sinful mankind (Exod. 31:13). As you study, take comfort in the fact that "if we confess our sins, He is faithful and just to forgive our sins and cleanse us from all unrighteousness" (1 John 1:9). Throughout the next two weeks, ask the LORD Our Sanctifier to grow love in your heart for YHWH Mekaddishkem as He reveals to you your utter need for Himself in order to be made holy in the eyes of God. Ask the LORD to help you prioritize the things that He reveals are important to His heart.

MONDAY AND TUESDAY (DAYS 1 AND 2): SABBATH COVENANT

The first passage we will study is a portion of a large section in Exodus devoted to the building of the Tabernacle and the artifacts associated with the Tabernacle based upon the instructions the LORD spoke to Moses as He met with Him on Mount Sinai. We find in Exodus 25:8-9 that the Tabernacle was a sovereign, divine plan rather than a longing in the heart of men. In YHWH Mekaddishkem's great love, He chose to have a sanctuary made so that he would "dwell in their midst" (Exod. 25:8). The LORD desired to meet with Moses and future high priests to speak with them and give them commandments for the people of Israel" (Exod. 25:21-22). He desired to be near to His people. This is astounding knowing that YHWH cannot be united with sin and must be completely separated from sin. In His design for the Tabernacle, this truth is reinforced by the veil of separation that is referred to as the "most holy place" where YHWH dwelt. By His own power, He enabled the Israelites to obey His instructions for building the Tabernacle; therefore, it was His might and wisdom alone that can be attributed to the creation of everything associated with the Tabernacle. "I have given to all able men ability, that they may make all that I have commanded you: the tent of meeting, and the ark of the testimony, and the mercy sea that is on it, and all the furnishings of the tent ..." (Exod. 31:6-10).

Not only did the LORD have specific building instructions, but the LORD Who Makes Holy had specific instructions regarding the conduct of the Israelites, particularly in regard to the Sabbath day. In Exodus 20:8-11, the Israelites were commanded to keep the Sabbath day holy as the fourth commandment. "The LORD blessed the Sabbath day and made it holy" (Exod. 20:11). In the upcoming passages, we will find that the Sabbath is exceedingly important to YHWH Mekaddishkem. Keeping the Sabbath is an avenue through which the LORD's people come to know Him as The LORD Our Sanctifier. The entire Sabbath law was created by YHWH to help His people understand the aspect of His unfailing character — He is the One Who Makes Holy sinful people so that He can dwell in their midst. The creation of the Tabernacle reminds us that even when we don't choose God or draw near to Him, God chooses to draw near to us. As YHWH draws near to a person, His very presence demands sanctification. Without His initiative in sanctification, all men and women would be desperately lost and far from YHWH.

READ EXODUS 25:8-9.
What reason does the LORD give for Tabernacle construction?

What does this statement reveal about the LORD's desires?

READ EXODUS 26:31-35.

List as many details about the veil that you can find.

What was the purpose of the veil? (See also, Ezek. 42:20, 44:23.)

Special Note: The Day of Atonement was the only exception for someone entering the holy of holies without facing immediate death (Lev. 16:2). The high priest would enter on this day after a purification offering (Lev. 16:11) and blood was sprinkled on the mercy seat (Lev. 16:14) as the high priest met with YHWH.

What does the veil reveal about the nature of YHWH and the nature of people?

What happened to the veil after Jesus' death on the cross? (See also, Matt. 27:50-54.)

What are the implications of the death of Jesus
in regard to the separation between holy YHWH
and sinful people? (See also, Heb. 10:19-22.)

READ EXODUS 31:1-11
What did the LORD call Bezalel, Oholiab, and
the able men to do in and for the Tabernacle?

How did YHWH equip them to carry out these tasks?

Use a dictionary and write the
definition of "sanctify" below.

In what ways is The LORD Who Sanctifies
You at work in this passage of Scripture?

What evidence do you find in Scripture of God's Sovereignty regarding the Tabernacle's creation?

Special Note: The phrase "dwelt among us" can also be translated as "tabernacled."

READ JOHN 1:14.
How does Jesus' presence on the earth reveal the LORD's nature as the One who draws near to make holy?

READ EXODUS 31:12-18
In this group of verses, how many times are the Israelites commanded to keep the Sabbath?

List a few of the ways this command is worded in Scripture.

List the reasons the LORD gives
for Sabbath day observance.

What words does the LORD use to
describe the Sabbath day?

*Special Note: The LORD compares the Sabbath covenant
to His day of rest after He created the world in six days.*

How do you think the observance of the Sabbath
sets-apart (sanctifies, makes holy) the Israelites
and brings glory to God through observance?

How do you think the Israelites keeping the Sabbaths
relates to "The LORD Who Sanctifies You?"

As the LORD Who Makes Holy gave directions in regard to the Tabernacle, He revealed His desire to be close to His people. Do you have a desire to be with your God? The LORD who has need of nothing, wants to dwell with those made in His image for His glory. As mankind is incapable of sinlessness, they are incapable of being near to the Holy, Holy, Holy; therefore, a veil of His design separated mankind from His presence as He dwelled within their camp. YHWH Mekaddishkem created a sacrificial and cleansing system that would provide atonement for sins so that sinful people could remain near the presence of God. He ordained the creation of the Tabernacle as an act of love for those He chose to draw near to as they obeyed His commands. His presence and plan made holy His people. The Tabernacle is a picture that points to Jesus Christ. As the Tabernacle was God's way of drawing near to men and making them holy, Jesus came and tabernacled among mankind and provided the way for us to be made holy before God forever. At Jesus' death, the veil that separated YHWH from His people was torn in two. Jesus entered as the Great High Priest the Most Holy Place once for all to make the fully sufficient sacrifice for sins (Heb. 9:12). Jesus' sacrificial death atoned for the sins of all who will come to Him so that they can experience freedom from sin; therefore, boldly approach YHWH (Heb. 10:19).

Additionally, when the LORD said to Moses that the Israelites were commanded to keep His Sabbaths "above all," it becomes clear that the LORD takes seriously and personally the Sabbath days. He calls it "a covenant forever" (Exod. 31:16) and "a sign between me and the people of Israel" (Exod. 31:17). God honors the day and sanctifies His people so that they can keep the Sabbath and honor the sign between God and man. In this passage we find that this covenant was yet another sanctifying act of mercy because in making the Sabbath, the LORD set apart a people for Himself. He did not allow for excuses in breaking the Sabbath covenant because it was truly established for the glory of God and the good of His people. "If you turn back your foot from the Sabbath, from doing your pleasure on my holy day, and call the Sabbath a delight and the holy day of the Lord honorable; if you honor it, not going your own ways, or seeking your own pleasure, or talking idly; then you shall take delight in the Lord, and I will make you ride on the heights of the earth; I will feed you with the heritage of Jacob your father, for the mouth of the Lord has spoken" (Isa. 58:13-14).

As the Israelites obeyed the LORD, they showed their devotion and obedience to the One who makes them holy. The other side of this statement is that if God was not YHWH Mekaddishkem, then the Israelites would have no hope in being able to obey and show devotion to the LORD Who Sanctifies. The people who honor the Sabbath and keep it holy are the ones who have been sanctified by The LORD Who Makes Holy. Ask the LORD Our Sanctifier to make you holy in Him. Stand on the verse that states that because of YHWH Mekaddishkem you are a part of the family of God: "Both the one who makes people holy and those who are made holy are of the same family. So, Jesus is not ashamed to call them brothers and sisters" (Heb. 2:11.)

WEDNESDAY AND THURSDAY (DAY 3 AND 4): SABBATH AND SANCTIFICATION

In Exodus 31, we studied the LORD Who Sanctifies alongside His Sabbath Covenant with His people, the Israelites. As we continue to look at the Sabbath and how it relates to YHWH Mekaddishkem's sanctifying work in our lives, we must keep in mind that God was the first to honor the Sabbath. After creating the universe in six days, he rested on the seventh. On the seventh day of Creation's existence, YHWH "blessed the seventh day and made it holy" (Gen. 2:4). Later, as God wrote with His finger the fourth of the Ten Commandments on a stone tablet, He instituted an unending command of Sabbath observance: "Remember the Sabbath day, to keep it holy. Six days you shall labor, and do all of your work, but the seventh day is a Sabbath to the LORD your God ... (Exod. 20:8-9). Clearly, the Sabbath matters to YHWH Mekaddishkem; therefore, it should matter to Christians enough to observe. Yet, Jesus and the New Testament writers had more to say about the Sabbath observance.

We find in Scriptures such as Romans 14:5 and Galatians 4:10 that Sabbath observance according to the Mosaic law is not a requirement for the New Testament church. For example: Modern day Christians celebrate the Sabbath on a Sunday because Jesus rose from the dead on a Sunday. Christians must guard against legalism regarding church attendance and rituals, but the act of setting aside one day out of the week to worship YHWH, study His Word, and rest from the demands of the world sets Christians apart as holy — the ones He sanctifies. When we honor the Sabbath, it is a sign that YHWH Mekaddishkem is doing His work within a believer. As we set aside one day out of the week for the

LORD Who Makes Holy, we are demonstrating our allegiance to Jesus as the One who has imputed His righteousness upon us and has made us holy by making us new creations in Christ.

Choosing a lifestyle in which we organize our weeks around worshipping and growing in our relationship with Jesus as a part of a body of believers is a sign of lifestyle devotion to YHWH Mekaddishkem. Additionally, as you prioritize obedience to the fourth commandment, your life becomes a testimony to unbelievers. As you sacrifice and turn down offers to participate in certain activities on the LORD's Day, people will ask questions. Then, you will be gifted with the opportunity to share that the LORD created everything in six days and then rested on the seventh. You will be able to explain why the LORD Our Sanctifier is worthy of a day devoted to His worship and glory. As you study the passages of Scripture this week, remember that when we make holy the Lord's Day by giving him the priority over all else, YHWH Mekaddishkem is at work within us.

READ ISAIAH 56:6-8.
What do these verses reveal about the Sabbath covenant in regard to foreigners (those that are not Israelites)?

READ ISAIAH 58:13-14.
From the verses, what behaviors please the LORD?

READ MARK 2:23 - 3:6.

What do you think Jesus meant whenever he said, "The Sabbath was made for man, not man for the Sabbath" (Mark 2:27)?

Ultimately, who is in charge of the Sabbath and the ways in which it should be observed?

Why were the Pharisees angry with Jesus?

Why was Jesus angry with the Pharisees?

What lessons did Jesus teach about Sabbath observance?

READ HEBREWS 10:19-25.

What encouragement is given in Hebrews 10:19-22 that might spur believers to draw near to God?

How might "not neglecting to meet together" (vs. 25) encourage other believers to walk in "love and good works" (vs. 24)?

What are the reasons provided for believers continuing to meet together?

What Scriptures remind you of YHWH Mekaddishkem who sanctifies (makes holy) His people?

Do you need to make changes to your weekly schedule to obey the LORD's commands and honor YHWH Mekaddishkem? If so, explain.

Have you observed any consequences in your life or the lives of fellow believers when the Sabbath has been neglected? If so, explain.

The Sabbath Day was made for man (Mark 2:27) and the glory of the LORD; therefore, it is for our benefit — benefits that are both spiritual and physical. In Isaiah 56, we find that in His love, the LORD even allowed foreigners to enter into a loving, covenant relationship with Himself while honoring the Sabbath. In Isaiah 58, we find that blessings such as riding "on the heights of the earth" and being fed "with the heritage of Jacob" are for the ones that "call the Sabbath a delight and the holy day of the LORD honorable" (vs. 14). In Mark 2 and 3, Jesus helps us understand that He is the Lord of the Sabbath, and it is honoring to God to do good on the Lord's Day. In Hebrews 10, we find evidence of the LORD Who Makes Holy as He encourages the Church to continue to meet together regularly so that God's set apart will be encouraged, stirred to act lovingly, encouraged to perform good works, and reminded of truths about Jesus Christ. With these truths in mind, is the regular gathering of believers a priority in your life?

Although the Word is clear, one day is not better than another (Rom. 14:5), God set a pattern for weekly observance of a Sabbath at creation. To neglect the fourth commandment and YHWH Mekaddishkem's eternal covenant is not without great consequence to our physical and spiritual health. What is holding you back from organizing your entire week around the things that honor God? Today, ask the LORD Who Makes Holy to sanctify you by His Spirit and power. Remember, "… there remains a Sabbath rest for the people of God, for whoever has entered God's rest has also rested from his works as God did from His. Let us therefore strive to enter that rest, so that no one may fall by the same sort of disobedience" (Heb. 4:9-11).

FRIDAY (DAY 5): REFLECTION

As you reflect upon the past week of Bible study, prayerfully and honestly answer the following questions.

How would you sum up the connection between YHWH Mekaddishkem (The LORD Who Sanctifies) and regular Sabbath observance?

How has the LORD Who Makes Holy sanctified you through regularly meeting with a body of believers to study His Word and worship His holy name?

Write a prayer of Thanksgiving to Jesus, the Lord of the Sabbath, for the gift of the Sabbath.

Obeying YHWH is usually costly. Read and reflect upon Luke 14:25-33. What might it cost you to obey the LORD by honoring the sabbath day and keeping it holy? Are you willing to choose obedience knowing the potential cost?

MONDAY AND TUESDAY (DAY 6 AND 7): THE LORD WHO SANCTIFIES YOU

Throughout the next two days, we will be looking at two select passages in Leviticus in which the LORD refers to Himself as YHWH Mekaddishkem and an additional passage regarding the Lord Who Sanctifies You's command that the Israelites be holy. The content within the book of Leviticus was given by God shortly after the construction of the Tabernacle, and Leviticus is often thought of as a continuation of Exodus's tabernacle commands. In this book, both ritual and ethical commands were given by the LORD to the Israelites. In detail, the Holy One outlines His standards for holy living. This book deals largely with identifying sin and addressing how the Israelites were to deal with sin so that the LORD could dwell among His people. We find in Leviticus 1:1 that God was present among His people. His presence was in the "tent of meeting" where He spoke to Moses regarding all that is written in Leviticus. His presence demanded that they strive to meet the LORD's holy standards.

In several places throughout the book of Leviticus, the LORD continues to reveal Himself as the One who sanctifies His people. He makes them holy, sets them apart, and calls them to lifestyles of holiness. It is only in relationship with YHWH Mekaddishkem that people are able to reflect His character as holy. According to Romans 7:18, nothing good dwells in a human. As totally depraved outside of Christ, we might have the desire to do what is right, but not the ability to carry it out without the sanctifying nature of YHWH present in our lives. YHWH urges His people, by

His own sanctifying power, to dedicate themselves to holy behavior and practices. Because "there is one God and there is one mediator between God and men, the man Christ Jesus" (1 Tim. 2:5), ask Jesus, through the power of the Holy Spirit indwelling all believers, to open and prepare your heart to His sanctifying work. He is YHWH Mekaddishkem. He alone is the One Who Makes Holy; therefore, pray "Is there any offensive way in me?" If so, LORD, "lead me in the way everlasting" (Ps. 139:24).

Special Note: Molech was a pagan false god to which worshippers would sacrifice their children as acts of worship and devotion.

READ LEVITICUS 20:1-9.
What were some of the practices that the LORD condemned as wicked? (For more sins, see also, Lev. 20:10-21.)

Do you find any evidence of the same types of sins in our culture today? If so, explain.

What were the punishments for the various crimes?

Summarize Leviticus 20:7-8 in your own words.

Describe the relationship between the LORD's sanctifying power and human responsibility. (See also, Phil. 2:12-13.)

READ LEVITICUS 20:22-26.
Record the different phrases that YHWH Mekaddishkem uses when He calls His people to holiness.

Why do you think that the LORD commanded that the Israelites be "separated from the peoples" and "not walk in the customs of the nations" that God was driving out?

In verse 26, what reason does the YHWH Mekaddishkem give for separating the Israelites from other people?

READ LEVITICUS 22:31-33.
What reason does the LORD provide for obedience to His commands?

How might disobedience to His commands "profane" His holy name: YHWH Mekaddishkem?

How does living obediently to the LORD's commands "sanctify" or "make holy" God among the people of Israel?

How might focusing Israel's attention on how YHWH brought them out of Egypt remind the Israelites that He makes them holy/set-apart?

In these passages, we uncover severe punishments for a variety of sinful activity. Studying God's wrath against sin might stir up feelings of discomfort and confusion regarding the severity He displays against sin. We, who daily experience the tension between our sinful flesh and the Spirit, tend to focus on the attributes of God that makes us feel better (His love, mercy, and goodness) while neglecting to focus on the attributes that cause us to tremble. The truth is that God takes sin seriously. "There is none holy like the LORD." There is no one that comes close to His measure of holiness (1 Sam. 2:2). In His holiness, He is completely just; therefore, His judgments against sin are righteous. The wages of sin, any sin, is death. Death is the just punishment from a holy God for wicked sinners (Rom. 6:23). In the passages studied, we found that God commands that His people keep "all statutes" and "all rules" (Lev. 20:22), but in Romans 3:23, Paul declares that "all have sinned" and no one can live up to the holiness standard of God. At this point, the news is very bad for mankind.

Because of these truths, James writes to sinners, "be wretched and mourn and weep" in regard to our sinfulness against the LORD (James 4:9). Since the LORD takes sin seriously, we should take sin seriously, too. We take sin seriously by truly admitting, mourning, and grieving our sin knowing that it grieves the heart of YHWH Mekaddishkem. We take sin seriously by confessing our sins to our brothers and sisters in Christ so that they can pray for us to be healed (James 5:16) and by allowing select, trusted friends the ability to lovingly correct us whenever they see something in our lives that doesn't align with the will of God. As the enemy attacks and tempts the people of God, we are called to offensively resist the Devil and draw near to God (James 4: 7-9). Thankfully, YHWH does not give us what we deserve (death for our sins). His grace is scandalous in light of his complete holiness and justice. He gives more grace to those who have humbled themselves before Himself by admitting their need for a rescue from the wrath of God against their sinfulness (James 4:6)!

All praise to YHWH Mekaddishkem (The LORD Who Makes Holy) for making, by His own power and might, a holy, set-apart people. In 1 Peter 2:9 Christians are called "a chosen race, a royal priesthood, a holy nation, a people for his own possession." Is this by their own doing? Of course not. It is only through His unending holiness and power that the Holy God sets apart a people and strengthens them to walk in holiness. It is because of His identity that He can command: "You shall be holy, for I am holy" (Isa. 6:3). He severs a people out for His own possession so that they would be His forever and He would be their God. Every act of sanctification that YHWH Mekaddishkem works in a believer is by His grace and mercy alone. Today, praise YHWH Mekaddishkem for sending Jesus to be the atoning sacrifice for your sins so that by grace through faith you might become a child of God. Follow the model of the psalmist, "I acknowledged my sin to you, and I did not cover my iniquity; I said, 'I will confess my transgressions to the LORD,' and you forgave the iniquity of my sin. Selah" (Ps. 32:5). Every day, remember that He gives grace to His people as they choose to humble themselves before the LORD, admitting their sins, and actively seeking to walk in obedience and repentance.

WEDNESDAY AND THURSDAY (DAY 8 AND 9): POSITIONAL AND PRACTICAL SANCTIFICATION

Sanctification (to be set apart or made holy) happens in two main ways. The first type of sanctification is positional in nature. One becomes sanctified and justified when they are washed in the blood of the Lamb at Salvation by the Spirit of God. 1 Corinthians 6:11 tells us that we are washed, sanctified, and justified in the name of the Lord Jesus by the Spirit of God at salvation. Men and women cannot take credit for their positional sanctification because the LORD chose people in Himself before the foundations of the world with the purpose of making them holy and blameless before Himself. He did this out of love (Eph. 1:4). Without this type of holiness, no human would ever be able to see the LORD (Heb. 12:14).

The second form of sanctification is ongoing in nature as the Holy Spirit matures one in Christ. As one grows in their relationship with Jesus and understanding of His Word, He prunes and refines them so that they grow in obedience to His commands and find freedom from sins in which they were once enslaved. The LORD Our Sanctifier is still responsible for practical sanctification within a believer, but He invites believers to be a part of the process as they respond to the Holy Spirit's revealing of sins, mourn their sins, and repent of their sins. It is through the process of practical sanctification that believers are able to keep themselves from being conformed into the image and patterns of the sinful world; therefore, they are able to present themselves as living sacrifices to God. As a believer undergoes practical sanctification, YHWH will declare His people as holy and acceptable in His sight (Rom. 12:1-2). Today, ask YHWH Mekaddishkem to sanctify you in truth because His Word is truth (John 17:17) as you study positional and practical sanctification. If you ask the LORD to sanctify you, He might take you on a journey that is uncomfortable. He might expose sin-sickness in your life that you didn't know was hidden within. He knows you better than you know yourself. Although the journey of practical sanctification might be painful, it will be fruitful and produce freedom in your life for the glory of YHWH, your Savior.

Positional Sanctification
READ 2 CORINTHIANS 5:14-21.

According to verse 17, describe what happens to a believer upon Salvation.

According to verse 18, who receives credit for the work done within a Christian?

What does it mean to be reconciled to God?

How is one able to become the "righteousness of God?"

How do you think this passage relates to YHWH Mekaddishkem, the LORD Who Makes Holy?

Positional and Practical Sanctification
READ HEBREWS 10:1-17.

What were the law, sacrifices, and sin offerings powerless to do in the life of one who had chosen to draw near to God?

What was the will of God?

How have Christians been sanctified (made holy)?

Describe the differences between the priestly sacrificial duties and the sacrifice of Christ Jesus?

In verse 14, we see both positional sanctification and practical sanctification. Which part of the verse points to positional sanctification, and which part of the verse points to practical sanctification?

How does the Holy Spirit help us grow in holiness/sanctification (vs. 16)?

Practical Sanctification
READ JOHN 15:1-5.

Who is the "True Vine?" Who is the "Vinedresser?"

How does the Vinedresser respond to a branch in Christ that does not bear fruit? How does this relate to the sanctifying work that the Father does in a Christian?

How is a Christian able to bear fruit?

In order to bear fruit, what is the responsibility of the believer?

Both positional and practical sanctification occur within a believer by the power of the Holy Spirit. The Holy Spirit baptizes believers into the body of Christ at Salvation (1 Cor. 12:13), and by Jesus' atoning sacrifice, the Holy Spirit makes holy those who have been chosen by God for salvation. It was and continues to be the will of God that Christians are set apart and declared holy and righteous by YHWH Mekaddishkem. Their status of "holy" is not by their own works but by grace through faith in Jesus' sacrifice for sins. The Holy Spirit is the one that makes a Christian holy as he or she receives the blood atonement of Jesus and His imputed righteousness. Today, praise YHWH Mekaddishkem for making you holy and giving you an underserved status that reflects His nature: holy. Because of Jesus, you can rightly say of yourself, "I'm holy in Christ!"

We who have been sanctified are not left powerless to continue in sin. The Holy Spirit convicts a believer of sin and transforms believers to become more like Jesus (2 Cor. 3:18). As we rely on YHWH Mekaddishkem to reveal our sin, He is faithful to cleanse us. He prunes us when we do not bear fruit so that we can walk in good works and righteousness. His pruning in your life might involve Him leading you to let go of a sinful relationship, leave a position, or cut out something you love that doesn't produce the fruit of the Spirit in your life. The process of practical sanctification is ongoing, costly, and painful as a believer mourns their sins against their Savior and LORD. Jesus explains the cost of being a true disciple: "If anyone would come after me, let him deny himself and take up his cross and follow me" (Matt. 16:24), yet Christians are not left without comfort.

Conviction of sin is a clear sign of the Holy Spirit's work within a believer, and we can take comfort in the fact that YHWH Mekaddishkem disciplines and reveals sin because He loves His children (Heb. 12:6). As you wrestle and struggle with sin, remember that the present sufferings associated with holy living are not worth comparing to the coming glory that will be revealed within each believer in Heaven (Rom. 8:18). Whatever you give up or walk away from on the earth for the sake of Christ will be such a small sacrifice compared to the treasure that awaits the faithful in Heaven. Allow your struggle with sin to produce within you excitement for your glorification one day in Christ.

FRIDAY (DAY 10): REFLECTION

As you reflect upon the past week of Bible study, prayerfully and honestly answer the following questions.

What sinful behaviors or thought processes has the Holy Spirit convicted you of throughout the past two weeks?

Write a prayer of thanksgiving to YHWH Mekaddishkem for setting you apart, making you holy, and sanctifying you.

How does knowing your identity in Christ as "holy" or "set-apart" affect your lifestyle?

In James 4:7, Christians are commanded to "resist the devil." The word for "resist" in the Greek is "antistēte," which means to "set against" or "withstand." This is a word that indicates completely standing against something while holding one's ground and refusing to be pushed backward towards retreat or loss. In Ephesians 6:11, Christians are commanded to "put on the whole armor of God [so that they] may be able to stand against the schemes of the devil." Only one offensive weapon is listed as a part of the Christian's armor — the sword of the Spirit which is the Word of God" (Eph. 6:17). We completely stand against the devil by offensively using the Word of God. With this in mind, list out habitual sins that you have been tolerating in your life. Look up verses to help you "resist the devil" and wield the sword of the Spirit by recording them below.

LESSON 5: YHWH SHALOM, THE LORD IS PEACE

The fifth compound name of the LORD, YHWH Shalom, occurs in Judges 6:24. Shalom means peace. "Shalom" is a common word used among Jews for both greetings and farewells, but "shalom," when attached to the LORD's personal name, refers to perfect, never-ending, and fully sufficient peace because the LORD Himself is holy, infinite, and sufficient for our every need. We find in Isaiah 9:6 that the Savior, Jesus, is named the Prince of Peace, and in regard to His peace, "there will be no end" (Isa. 9:7). Surprisingly, it is Gideon, a judge of Israel who significantly contributed to Israel's continued downward spiral of abandonment and renunciation of the LORD (Judg. 8:22-28), who attributed "peace" to the LORD's name. The LORD called upon Gideon to deliver the Israelites out of the oppression from the Midianites; therefore, he built an altar to the LORD and called it, "The LORD Is Peace." Although Gideon had many fears, he was obedient to the LORD in regard to Israel's deliverance from their enemies and earned His name listed among the heroes of faith in Hebrews 11.

In the book of Judges, where we find the use of "The LORD Is Peace," Israel is caught in a cycle of apostasy, servitude, repentance, and salvation. Before the rise of each judge, Israel acted wickedly and played the harlot with false gods. In punishment, the LORD determined that His people would be overtaken by a surrounding enemy and oppressed for a time. Due to their oppression, the Israelites cried out to God for deliverance. Each time, the LORD raised up a judge to save His people only for them to fall back into their wicked ways. At the start of each new cycle, Israel stoops into increasingly worse depravity as their disobedience becomes more serious against God. The entire book of Judges seems to describe a nation that is in absolute chaos — a nation that is in desperate need of the LORD Is Peace. We clearly find that God is too merciful to allow His people to continue in their disobedience; therefore, He allows them to suffer the consequences of their apostasy. Disobedience destroys peace. There is no peace whenever idolatry is present because a man-made god is incapable of peace.

Every person can relate to the nation of Israel. We are all prone to fall into cycles of sin that threaten our peace. We all face circumstances that tempt us toward despair and doubt in regard to the character of God. No matter the cause of our anxiousness and unrest, the LORD is faithful to infinitely provide His peace to His people. All glory and praise to the LORD because He is YHWH Shalom despite our feelings and personal experiences. The LORD is our only hope for having a relationship with God and true peace in a chaotic, fallen world. In the midst of chaos and trauma, you can rest in the reality that "the peace of God, which surpasses all understanding, will guard your hearts and minds in Christ Jesus" if you are truly His child (Phil. 4:7). Over the next two weeks, as you study YHWH Shalom, ask the Holy Spirit to help you recognize that the LORD leads His people beside still waters, restores souls, leads down paths of righteousness, comforts with His leadership and discipline, and is ever-present when His people are experiencing evil (Ps. 23).

MONDAY AND TUESDAY (DAY 1 AND 2): THE LORD IS PEACE

After the death of Moses, the LORD chose Joshua to command and lead the Israelites. Joshua led the Israelites in many battles as they conquered pagan nations to inherit the Promise Land. Once Joshua died, the Israelites disobeyed the command of the LORD and failed to completely drive out the inhabitants of the nations they were to inherit. Instead, they chose to keep people as forced labor which was contrary to the LORD's will. Their incomplete conquests were the foundation to their great falling away from the LORD because by allowing the inhabitants of the pagan nations to remain among them, they surrounded themselves with the worship of other gods and wicked culture. We are not to be deceived, "bad company ruins good morals" (1 Cor. 15:33).

Eventually the Israelites began to worship other gods and engage in great evil. "And the people of Israel did what was evil in the sight of the LORD and served the Baals. They abandoned the LORD, the God of their fathers, who had brought them out of the land of Egypt" (Judg. 2:11-12). Because of this, the LORD "gave them over to plunderers" and "He sold them into the hand of their surrounding enemies" causing His people to be in great distress (Judg. 2:14). The LORD Is Peace raised up judges to save His people, but the people continued to worship other gods and turn away from the One Who Is Peace. YHWH raised up Othniel, Ehud, and Deborah and each time after the judge delivered the Israelites from oppression, the Israelites turned back to their evil. The LORD Is Peace provided commands that if obeyed, would have brought peace to the Israelites. Instead of trusting the One who brings peace because He is Peace, they wallowed in disobedience that resulted in physical unrest and inner turmoil. Do we not do the same? As we come to know the LORD Is Peace, we are more likely to follow His leadership because we trust that His actions produce Peace in our anxious, weary hearts.

Over the next two days, we will be studying the oppression of Israel by the Midianites, the call of Gideon, the destruction of the altars of Baal, and Gideon's Fleece test all found in Judges chapter 6. As you study, ask YHWH Shalom to reveal to you His peace in the midst of turmoil. Ask the LORD to reveal ways in which you have chosen to reject YHWH Shalom's leadership toward peace and chosen to go your own way.

READ JUDGES 6:1-10.
Since the LORD Is Peace, what does this reveal about His commands?

Why might doing what is evil in the sight of the LORD hinder peace?

Can you think of a time that your disobedience resulted in a lack of peace in your life?

Describe the oppression of the Israelites.

According to verse 1, who was responsible for the Israelites oppression by the Midianites?

How did the Israelites respond to being humbled by the Midianites?

In your own words, what did the LORD say through the prophet to Israel after they cried out to Him for help?

What aspects of the LORD's words
point to His nature as Peace?

How might idolatry and disobedience
result in a lack of peace?

READ JUDGES 6:11-24.
How does the LORD refer to Gideon in verse 12?

How would you describe Gideon based
upon his responses to the LORD?

How did Gideon feel about Himself
according to verse 15?

What encouragement did the LORD offer to Gideon in verse 16?

What sign did the angel of the LORD provide in order to convince Gideon that he was in the presence of the angel of the LORD?

Why did Gideon build an altar?

Why do you think he named the altar, "The LORD Is Peace?"

What aspects of this passage point to the LORD's character as Peace?

The LORD Is Peace gave the Israelites peace from the bondage of the Egyptians and granted them victory over the nations that inhabited the Promised Land. Despite the peace offered, the Israelites chose to worship the gods of the Amorites and Midianites. They turned to gods that could never bring peace to their souls; therefore, the LORD gave them over to the unrest that they chose. The Israelites quickly learned that false gods are powerless. When they cried out to YHWH in desperation, He heard their cries and responded in order to bring them back into step with Himself — their source of peace. YHWH Shalom is faithful to hear from Heaven, forgive sins, and heal lands whenever His people humble themselves, pray, seek His face, and turn from their wickedness (2 Chron. 7:14).

In response to His peoples' cries, the LORD Is Peace chose an unlikely and quite fearful deliverer for the Israelites. Gideon belonged to the weakest clan in Manasseh, and he was considered least in his father's household. He was full of doubts about the goodness and presence of God due to the oppression from the Midianites. Gideon had to be convinced that the one to which He spoke was truly the angel of the LORD. Despite all of these things, the LORD called him a "mighty man of valor" (Judg. 6:12) and spoke powerful words to him: "Peace be to you. Do not fear; you shall not die" (Judg. 6:23). Gideon and the angel of the LORD's conversation began with questions and accusations against the LORD, but when Gideon built an altar to the LORD, he was sure of the truth: The LORD Is Peace. Throughout the LORD's patient dealings with Gideon, we find that the LORD Is Peace often chooses unlikely candidates, takes them out of their comfort zones, and uses them for His purposes all while strengthening, encouraging, and reassuring them of His faithfulness and goodness.

All of the turmoil and trauma that Gideon and the other Israelites had endured at the hands of the Midianites would come to an end. Their suffering and oppression would end not because of their own efforts and worth but because YHWH is Shalom. He is peace. While there was once enmity between the Israelites and the LORD due to their idolatry and wickedness, the LORD drew His people back to Himself with strong discipline so that they might once again experience peace by being in a right relationship with YHWH Shalom. As we relate this passage to our lives remember the Prince of Peace: While we were at enmity with God, Jesus became our peace. By giving His life, he reconciled us to God and put to death the sin barrier that stood between God and man. "For He Himself is our peace, who made both groups (Jews and Gentiles) into one and broke down the barrier of the dividing wall, by abolishing in His flesh the enmity, which is the Law of commandments contained in ordinances, so that in Himself He might make the two into one new man, thus establishing peace, and might reconcile them both in one body to God through the cross, by it having put to death the enmity" (Eph. 2:14-16). All glory to God!

WEDNESDAY AND THURSDAY (DAY 3 AND 4): THE LORD STILLS GIDEON'S FEARS

The LORD had revealed Himself to Gideon as Peace, but Gideon still wrestled with great fear and reluctance to both believe the words of the LORD and act accordingly. In the passages that we will study over the next two days, we will study the life of a man that was too afraid to destroy idols in the presence of his family and townsfolk, neglected to take pride in His actions of destroying Baal's altar and the Asherah by claiming responsibility, and tested the LORD twice before acting upon His commands. Although such testing of the LORD was condemned by the Mosaic Law which states: "You shall not put the LORD your God to the test" (Deut. 6:16), YHWH Shalom brought peace to Gideon by accommodating his requests.

As you study, ask The LORD Is Peace to reveal to you how idolatry, doubt, and faithlessness result in fear. Your idols might not be as apparent as statues and poles, but when the emotion of fear is present within a person, it often shines light on idols present in someone's' heart. Gideon feared His family's opinions; therefore, he idolatrized and worshiped the opinions of others. Gideon feared the consequences of righteousness; therefore, idolatrized his security and comfort. Gideon feared for His life; therefore, idolatrized and worshiped His God-given life more than the Giver. Though we are prone to idolatry and fear, like Gideon, YHWH Shalom is faithful to offer His peace to us by destroying our idols and extending His mercy to us whenever we fail to fully trust in His Words and Divine will. Both the Israelites' idols and our idols must be torn down. Because of the nature of YHWH, we are not enslaved to fear of man and the bondage of idolatry. As you study the LORD's care over Gideon as He calms Gideon's fears, let your heart be reminded that the Prince of Peace is ever-present and able to calm the fears within your heart and help you walk in obedience to His commands. Because YHWH is peace, ask Him to fill you will the peace that surpasses all understanding to guard your heart and mind (Phil. 4:7) as you seek to know Him and walk in obedience.

READ JUDGES 6:25-27.
What do these verses reveal about Gideon's father?

What did the LORD tell Gideon to do?

Why do you think Gideon might have been afraid of his family and the men of the town? (See also, Judg. 6:28-32.)

What was the response of Joash's men to Gideon's actions?

How does Joash seem to change in
light of his son's actions?

What was Gideon's new name?

What might Gideon's name continually
remind the Israelites of in regard to Baal?

READ JUDGES 6:33-40.
Describe the threat against God's
people. (See also, Judg. 6:3-4.)

How did the LORD equip Gideon
to deal with the threat?

How did Gideon respond?

Who enabled him to do so?

What might the two tests Gideon
set-up reveal about Gideon?

What do you think YHWH Shalom's response
to Gideon's tests reveal about God? (See
also, Exod. 34:6 and Neh. 9:16-17.)

In what ways has the LORD been patient
toward you and calmed your fears?

> What aspects of these passages point to YHWH Shalom and/or the rejection of His peace?

Gideon was a part of a household that was walking in direct opposition to The LORD Is Peace due to their worship of Baal and Asherah. There was great hostility between the people of Joash and the LORD Almighty, but rich in Mercy, the One who is peace commanded an act of destruction. As Gideon tore down the altar to Baal and the Asherah, built a new altar to the LORD, and sacrificed to the True God, the LORD Is Peace was reminding His people that He alone is worthy of their worship. While idolatry would lead them further into despair, the LORD sought them in their wickedness to offer Peace. The LORD would not allow His people to continue in their idolatry because there is unrest until one is in right relationship with Himself. Although Gideon acted in the dark because fear of man ruled in His heart, God used His obedience to bring His father back to the truth: Baal has no power because he is not a god. In application, our lifestyles of devotion and obedience to YHWH will likely have an impact on our family members. We must be mindful of our words and actions as we engage with our family members. Are we pointing our family members to or away from obedience to God?

Directly following the destruction of idolatry both physically and spiritually, the LORD Is Peace was at work as the Midianites and Amalekites planned another raid to devour the Israelites crops and livestock. When unrest and suffering seemed imminent and dread likely filled the Israelites, God clothed Gideon in His Spirit so that he would rally the tribes to fight for peace against their enemies. Peace must have seemed unbelievable to the Israelites' chosen deliverer, Gideon, because He wickedly tested God (Deut. 6:16) by asking for two signs to confirm words that the LORD had already spoken. Ever patient and long-suffering, the LORD grants Gideon's requests for signs. The peace from their enemies that the LORD had promised to grant the Israelites through Gideon's leadership would occur because The LORD is Peace had promised.

Before we judge Gideon and entertain thoughts of spiritual superiority, let us consider: Are we prone to neglect the words of the LORD, forget His promises, hand over our peace to embrace insecurities, and beg for reassurance of truths in which we should be already standing? Yes, of course. May we recognize how often we test the LORD and display weak faith by the power of the Holy Spirit so that we can repent. When we look closely into our behaviors, do we find ourselves reluctant to walk in boldness? As The LORD Is Peace graciously reassured Gideon and strengthened His faith, the LORD of peace is powerful to give you peace at all times and in every way as you reflect upon His Word and recognize that He has overcome the world.

FRIDAY (DAY 5): REFLECTION

As you reflect upon the past week of Bible study, prayerfully and honestly answer the following questions.

In what ways do you relate to Gideon?

How have you experienced YHWH Shalom in your life?

Read Philippians 4:6. Make a list of the circumstances in your life in which you feel anxious or worried. Starting with thanksgiving, write a prayer to present your requests to God.

MONDAY AND TUESDAY (DAY 6 AND 7): THE LORD IS PEACE'S PLAN

Jesus says, "blessed are the poor in spirit for theirs is the kingdom of heaven" (Matt. 5:3). His words remind us of the absolute importance of relying on the LORD alone and recognizing our dire need for God's help. Though we are spiritually bankrupt, we are prone to seek control and bestow ourselves the credit for our accomplishments. The Israelites were no different, and YHWH mercifully protected them from the spiritual danger of trusting in their own strength. As the Israelites prepared for war against the Midianites, Amalekites, and the people of the East whose numbers were compared to "locusts in abundance" and "their camels were without number, as the sand that is on the seashore" (Judg. 7:12), YHWH Shalom reduced their numbers to only 300 men. Why? So that Israel would be spared from boasting against God with statements such as "my own hand has saved me" (Judg. 7:2). YHWH Shalom was providing the Israelites with physical peace from the oppression of their enemies, but He was also guarding their hearts from worshiping themselves through claiming the credit for their victories and believing that they were their own heroes. Such pride and idolatry will never lead to peace between God and mankind; rather, pride proceeds destruction and a haughty spirit comes before a fall (Prov. 16:18).

Additionally, in this chapter, it is evident that Gideon's heart was still not at peace despite the LORD's promises and signs. Because He is the One who searches and knows the depths and thoughts of all, the LORD Is Peace patiently and graciously responded to Gideon's fears. YHWH

Shalom knows exactly the encouragement that we need and when we need it. In this passage, it is clear that Gideon had experienced enough to be fear-free in regard to the coming battle, but He was still afraid. The LORD Is Peace patiently met Gideon where he was at and led him into an experience that built courage within him. As you study Judges 7, ask the LORD Is Peace to reveal to you ways in which He was working among His people. Ask YHWH Shalom to remind you of His patience with you in the midst of your fears and to fill you with adoration for the way that He brings peace to your anxious heart and doesn't abandon you in your weakness. Remember, "God has not given us a spirit of fear, but of power, love, and self-control" (2 Tim. 1:7).

READ JUDGES 7:1-8.
What misconception was the LORD sparing the Israelites from by lowering the number of men to face the Midianites?

Why might the thought process: "my own hand has saved me," be dangerous and contrary to true peace?

What was the first strategy used to decrease the numbers of the Israelite camp?

How many soldiers were fearful?

Describe the second means through which the LORD decreased the numbers of the Israelite camp.

READ JUDGES 7:9-18.
What evidence do you find in Scripture that Gideon is still experiencing fear?

How does The LORD Is Peace respond to Gideon's fears?

Describe the dream that Gideon overheard two Midianites discussing.

What was Gideon's response to the LORD's orchestrated encouragement?

In what ways has the LORD stilled your fears in order to help you walk in obedience, boldness, and faith? In what ways is the LORD leading you to step out in obedience while trusting in Him alone?

READ JUDGES 7:19-25.
What was the responsibility of Gideon and the 300 men?

What miracles did YHWH accomplish in order to bring peace to the Israelites?

Using the Scriptures studied over the past two days, what key points reveal YHWH Shalom's nature?

Gideon's trust in God wavered as God forced the reduction of the Israelite army from 32,000 soldiers to 300, but he obeyed the LORD by sending all but a fraction of a percent of the army to their tents. As Gideon looked at the vast army that camped in the valley below him, he was afraid. Fear had been a trend in Gideon's life. In his fears, YHWH Shalom did not despise him. It is not recorded that Gideon cried out to the LORD or questioned His Divine plan after diminishing the army to only 300 soldiers, but the Prince of Peace determined to bless Gideon with His peace by telling Gideon to go down to the camp of his enemies in order to eavesdrop on a conversation. Gideon, probably quaking with fear, snuck to the outposts and overheard a dream which pointed to God giving Midian and their entire camp into the hands of Gideon. This was God's plan to strengthen Gideon's resolve and faith. As the LORD confirmed His promise, Gideon's fears were stilled, and Gideon worshiped. Gideon was humbled by the realization that the LORD was working in the camp of his enemies — even his enemies were dreaming and discussing the future victory of Gideon.

As we study the historic story of Gideon's defeat of the Midianites, it seems highly unlikely that Gideon would ever forsake YHWH. Ironically, the miraculous battle against the Midianites didn't include Gideon or the 300 Israelites. God Himself brought peace to the Israelites by causing the Midianites to run in fear as the 300 men stood in place. As the army fled, they turned their swords against their comrades, while the 300 men looked on with trumpets and torches in hands instead of spears and swords. YHWH Shalom caused chaos while Gideon and his men stood still in perfect peace as the LORD fought their battle for them. All victory belongs to the LORD — spiritual, emotional, and physical. May His name be forever lifted high!

Unfortunately, after Israel's victory over the Midianites, Gideon's heart did not reflect the peace of YHWH. Gideon and his 300 men pursued rogue missions that the LORD did not command. They engaged in military action against the kings of Midian — Zebah and Zalmunna, the army of the "people of the East" to which Zebah and Zalmunna had fled, and the men of Succoth and Penuel who denied Gideon and his army bread. His attitude during the events in Judges 8 reflected pride, brutality, and personal vengeance. Despite the LORD is Peace's faithfulness to Gideon and Israel, Gideon fell into apostasy himself as he caused the people of God to engage in idolatry. Gideon used the spoils of war to create an ephod (an ornate garment worn by the high priest). This ephod was placed in Gideon's city and "all Israel whored after it there, and it became a snare to Gideon and to his family" (Judg. 8:27). The end of Gideon's story is a sobering warning for us all. Whatever fame or success is given to us by YHWH is to be received humbly. We must give YHWH the glory for our accomplishments and guard our hearts and lives against idolatry. We must seek the LORD is Peace's will before engaging in any form of conflict. Today, ask the LORD to help you tear down any activities in your life that take the place of YHWH in your heart. Ask the LORD to keep you from engaging in actions apart from God's will. Doing what is right in our own eyes will surely never lead to peace.

WEDNESDAY AND THURSDAY (DAY 8 AND 9): NEW TESTAMENT PASSAGES ABOUT YHWH SHALOM

Over the next two days, we will be examining two different New Testament passages that point to YHWH Shalom's peace and implications on the lives of Christians. In the beginning of Ephesians 2, Paul described a person's condition outside of a relationship with Christ as dead — dead in sins and under the wrath of God. Then, Paul explained how people are saved by grace through faith and given a new position in relation to God the Father through Christ Jesus. Instead of separated from God due to sin, in Christ one is raised up and seated with Him in heavenly places. Jesus' death as an atoning sacrifice for our sins is how we are able to have peace with God. Since we have been granted peace with God, we are able to have peace with the body of Christ and God Himself.

The peace granted to us on behalf of Christ has many implications to our lives. We are promised tribulation, suffering, and many trials while living in the world, but Jesus reminds us to "take heart" because He has "overcome the world" (John 16:33). Thankfully, Jesus also promises Christians the gift of His infinite peace (John 14:27). These are the very truths that Christians can cling to while enduring sufferings. As we are tempted to forfeit the gift of peace in Christ, we should stand on the words and teachings of Jesus. As Jesus' peace is manifested in our lives, the watching world will note differences between their chaos and anxiety within trials versus the Christian's trust in their LORD. This will open doors to evangelism as the unbelieving world witnesses the difference that the Prince of Peace makes in the lives of His followers. Over the next two days, we will look closely at several passages that will help us understand how YHWH Shalom commands us to live in light of the peace we have due to the Prince of Peace, Jesus. His peace has practical implications in our lives, and obedience to His commands sets the stage for His peace to reign in our hearts and lives. Today, ask YHWH Shalom to show you His way of peace.

Special Note: In this section, we will focus on how Jesus, through His atoning death on the cross, made peace between Jews and Gentiles as the one body and church of God.

READ EPHESIANS 2:11-15.
What group of people is Paul speaking to in this passage?

Using verse 12, describe a Gentile's relationship to God and the people of God (Jews) before Jesus' work on the cross?

What does it mean to be brought near to God and how was this accomplished?

In what ways did the law bring hostility between Jews and Gentiles?

How does Jesus make peace between Jews and Gentiles?

Special Note: In this section of Scripture, we will focus on how God made peace between the unified church and Himself through Jesus.

READ EPHESIANS 2:16-18.
To whom did Jesus preach peace?

How does Jesus' work give us access to the Father?

In what ways does Jesus "reconcile to himself all things" and "make peace by the blood of his cross" (Col. 1:20) according to the Ephesians 2:11-18?

READ COLOSSIANS 3:1-17.
What are Christians called to seek and set their minds upon?

How might obedience to these commands produce peace in one's life?

What earthly/fleshly sins and desires do you struggle with regularly using the list of sins in Colossians 3?

In what ways do these sins hinder peace?

Focusing on verse 11, what mindset is required in the body of Christ?

How might this mindset produce unity and peace in a body of believers?

Using the lists of godly behavior in verses 12-14, choose three characteristics that Christians are commanded to "put on" and explain how doing so produces peace in relationships with others?

How do you think thankfulness causes peace to rule in one's heart?

Using the list of spiritual activities in verses 16-17, which acts do you need to focus on in order to walk in God's peace?

We find in Ephesians 2 that Jesus broke down the division of people as either Jews (God's people) or Gentiles (far off) and created the "the church of God" (1 Cor. 10:32). Now, both Jews and Gentiles have direct access to God through Christ's propitiation. Verse 14 tells us that Jesus is our peace between mankind and God and those within the global church. The Jews were set-apart by God through the observance of the Mosaic Law including circumcision and other rituals and ordinances. The Mosaic Law was a barrier for the Gentiles from entering into covenant with YHWH. Christ Jesus abolished in His own body the dividing wall between Gentiles and Jews by fulfilling the righteous requirements of the law (Matt. 5:17) and removed whoever believed, both Jew and Gentile, from the condemnation associated with breaking the law. This act created "one new man" which is anyone created new in Christ, in place of the two: Gentiles and Jews. Christ alone is able to accomplish peace between mankind and God and within the body of Christ.

In Colossians 3, all Christians are commanded to put the death their sinful behavior and desires and to "put on" compassionate hearts, kindness, humility, meekness, patience, forgivingness, and love. This passage describes the Biblical principle of replacement. As we recognize sins in our lives, we are to put them off and replace the sin by putting on attributes/actions pleasing to the LORD. This principle can also be applied to toxic thoughts. We are to "take captive " (2 Cor. 10:5) our sinful thoughts, and fill our minds with true, noble, right, pure, lovely, admirable, excellent, or praiseworthy things (Phil. 4:8). The peace of God will not be found in disobedience; rather, peace resides as one sets their intentions on seeking the LORD and His Will. As the holy and beloved of the Lord focus on behavior that lets the peace of Christ rule in their hearts, internal and external peace results.

As Jesus prepared His disciples for life without Him walking among them in the flesh, He said: "Peace I leave with you; my peace I give to you. Not as the world gives do I give to you. Let not your hearts be troubled, neither, let them be afraid" (John 14:27-28). To know Jesus is to know YHWH Shalom. His peace is among us. He has given us His peace at all times. It is our responsibility as believers indwelled by the Holy Spirit to let not our hearts be troubled or afraid. We do this by letting the word of Christ dwell within us, putting on harmonious behavior through His strength, putting off sinful thought processes and actions, and seeking Christ above all else as the Prince of Peace. Are you in need of His peace today? Take time to draw near to the Prince of Peace.

FRIDAY (DAY 10): REFLECTION

As you reflect upon the past week of Bible study, prayerfully and honestly answer the following questions.

> Hebrews 12:14 states: "Make every effort to live in peace with everyone and to be holy; without holiness no one will see the Lord." What practical changes do you need to make in your relationships in order to "live in peace with everyone?"

How do you think that these changes will help people "see the Lord" in your life?

Read 1 Peter 3:9-11. What aspects stand out to you from this passage?

In what ways can you practically walk out the commands within this passage? Explain.

LESSON 6: YHWH SABAOTH, THE LORD OF HOSTS

"For behold, He who forms mountains and creates the wind and declares to man what are His thoughts, He who makes dawn into darkness and treads on the high places of the earth, The Lord God of Hosts is His name" (Amos 4:13). This verse describes the stand-alone LORD of Hosts — The all-knowing Creator of both the seen and unseen. He knows the inner thoughts of men and woman, controls days and nights, and is above all in every way. The LORD of Hosts, also referred to as YHWH Sabaoth, will be the focus of our Bible study over the next two weeks. Sabaoth comes from the Hebrew word "tsaba", which means army, war, or warfare. There are many instances in the Word of God in which the word "sabaoth" is used in conjunction with YHWH as a proper noun. In this study of YHWH Sabaoth, we will look at several passages in which the LORD is named the LORD of Hosts!

The first use of YHWH Sabaoth is in the form of a prayer from a desperate, barren woman named Hannah. Hannah called upon the LORD of Hosts to grant her a child. Hannah believed that the LORD had all authority, power, and control; therefore, He was the only One able to control her ability to bear a child. Knowing YHWH controlled all of the armies of the universe, heaven, and earth, Hannah stood in faith upon the truth that YHWH certainly controls the conception of a child. David, who would later be titled "King David," regularly referred to YHWH as the LORD of Hosts. As David battled many foes and eventually rose to the station of King, He stood firm in the belief that it is only YHWH Sabaoth that brings about success in a person's life. As the LORD of Hosts used David in mighty ways and promised Him continued greatness, David remained humble as He continually focused on the sovereignty of the Almighty. In calling YHWH, the LORD of Hosts, David ascribed to the LORD all power and authority over Heaven, Earth, Hell, and everything in between. Both Hannah and David showed faith in the LORD of Hosts as the Supreme Authority, yet there is another aspect to the LORD's nature as Sabaoth.

Throughout the Word of God, Sabaoth is attached to the LORD's personal name to describe His justice and wrath poured out against wickedness. He determines all outcomes, and no one can stand against His vengeance. In all YHWH Sabaoth does, His character is unchanging as faithful and true. It is with justice that YHWH Sabaoth judges and makes war (Rev. 19:11). YHWH is 100 percent, infinitely wrathful against sin while being 100 percent, infinitely just. All the while being 100 percent, infinitely loving. His characteristics never contradict each other. While uncovering that the LORD of Host's wrath against sin is an infinite aspect of His unchanging character, Christians can take comfort in the fact that the LORD of Hosts, who had all power and right to annihilate all of mankind due to their sins, sent Jesus to die for the ungodly. This is how YHWH showed His immense love for sinners — Christ Jesus bore the wrath that their sins demanded (Rom. 5:6-8). When one comes to faith in Jesus as their Savior and Lord, they are no longer under the God of angel armies' wrath (Rom. 8:1).

Throughout these two weeks, declare the following Scripture: "Holy, Holy, Holy, is the Lord of hosts, The whole earth is full of His glory" (Isa. 6:3). In all YHWH Sabaoth does, He is absolutely holy. He acts out of His omnipotence, omniscience, and sovereignty as He says of Himself "I am the first and I am the last; beside me there is no god" (Isa. 44:6). As you study, ask the LORD to help you surrender control and worry as you come to know His nature as the LORD of Hosts.

MONDAY AND TUESDAY (DAY 1 AND 2): HANNAH, SAMUEL, AND THE LORD OF HOSTS

In James 1:2-4, we are commanded as the people of God to count our trials and sufferings as joy because the testing of our faith produces within a person what is needed to become more like Jesus. The command to count sufferings as joy does not indicate that the LORD expects His children to sweep their grief and sorrow under the rug and pretend as if their pain doesn't matter to YHWH. Jesus Himself was described prophetically as "a man of sorrows" who was "acquainted with grief" (Isa. 53:3). James describes trials as helpful to Christians in becoming "perfect and complete" and "lacking in nothing" (James 1:4). As we cry out to the LORD of Hosts as the one who has all authority, power, and control over the hosts of heaven, earth, and everything in between, we are turning to the only one with the ability to see us through the times of suffering and supernaturally provide us with His joy. He alone holds the power over the opposition in our lives. All authority is His to either keep us in our trial for His good purposes or to work mightily to bring about the freedom from the warfare we face. He will always do what is good, just, and perfect in every way. It is in realization of these truths that a Christian is able to relish in a fruit of the Spirit, joy, which comes from the LORD and is independent of circumstances.

Throughout the next two days, we will be studying a passage in which Hannah suffered for years. Her main trial, the inability to bear children, led to a ripple effect of other trials in her life. Her trials included barrenness in a culture that determined the value of a woman based upon their ability to bear children. Hannah's inability to bear an heir to carry on the family name and provide future security for the family most likely resulted in Elkanah taking a second wife, Peninnah. Peninnah, described as Hannah's rival (1 Sam. 1:6), used to "provoke [Hannah] grievously to irritate her." This grievous provoking was not a one-time event, but an occurrence that went on year after year. The one charged with causing Hannah's pain was not just Peninnah but the LORD because "the LORD had closed her womb" (1 Sam. 1:5). It was YHWH Sabaoth's will for Hannah to endure barrenness for a set time which resulted in incredible pain and longing.

Full-of-faith, Hannah called upon the LORD of Hosts. In doing so, she revealed that she had the faith in the one who has authority over all of the hosts of heaven and earth to powerfully create within her life for His glory and praise. Since YHWH Sabaoth controls all of the armies of the universe, heaven, and earth, He most certainly controls the conception of a child. In her pain, she called upon YHWH Sabaoth. Hannah likely felt as though she was in a war because she had a rival, Peninnah, who provoked her and irritated her due to the LORD's act of closing Hannah's womb. Additionally, Hannah was facing spiritual warfare as she was tempted to doubt the goodness, care, and sovereign plan of the LORD of Hosts. Hannah's trial grew her faith. After she received the promise from the LORD of Hosts and fulfilled her vow to Him, Hannah was able to declare "My heart exults in the LORD; my strength is exalted in the LORD" (1 Sam. 2:1). As you study, ask YHWH Sabaoth to reveal to you areas in your life in which you need to submit to His authority and all-powerful ability to control the times and seasons of your life. Then, choose to rest in His goodness and sovereignty knowing that His plans are to prosper and not to harm His children (Jer. 29:11).

READ 1 SAMUEL 1:1-8
Who is Elkanah worshipping and sacrificing to at Shiloh?

What indications do you find in Scripture that Elkanah loved Hannah more than Peninnah?

Describe the situation(s) that were afflicting Hannah and causing her suffering?

READ 1 SAMUEL 1:9-20.
To whom did Hannah call upon to help her in her distress?

In your own words, what vow did Hannah make to the LORD of Hosts?

After Eli wrongly judged Hannah as a drunken woman, how did Hannah describe her praying before the LORD?

How did the LORD of Hosts respond to Hannah's prayer and Eli's blessing?

READ 1 SAMUEL 1:21-27.
How did Hannah keep her vow to the LORD of hosts?

How can/should parents apply verses 27-28 to their own children's lives?

If you were Hannah, what emotions do you think that you would experience in fulfilling your vow to the LORD of hosts to lend/dedicate/give Samuel to the LORD of as long as Samuel lives?

READ 1 SAMUEL 2:1-10.
What aspects of Hannah's prayer indicate that she acknowledges the LORD of Host's power, authority, and control?

Overall, after giving her only son to the LORD, what was Hannah's emotional state?

What aspects of the Scripture study reveal the LORD's nature as the LORD of Hosts (controller of times, seasons, and armies)?

Samuel's name showed that Hannah believed that the LORD of Hosts commands all things — even the conception of children. Samuel's name means "name of God." Another possible definition of Samuel's name is "offspring of God" The idea is that Samuel bore the name of God because God had given him to Hannah out of His own power. Hannah vows to the LORD of Hosts: "I will give him (Samuel) to the LORD all the days of his life, and no razor shall touch His head" (1 Sam. 1:11). Hannah dedicated the child for which she deeply longed to the Victorious One to be a Nazarite and serve in the temple of the LORD for all of his days. Although Hannah only declared that a razor would not touch her son's hair, she likely spoke to the entire Nazarite vow outlined in Numbers 6. When one is under a Nazarite vow, he is set-apart unto the LORD and separated from the world which is evidenced through the avoiding of all food and drink coming from the grapevine, dead bodies, and the razor. She fully surrendered Samuel to YHWH Sabaoth. By surrendering control of her most precious gift, she demonstrated her faith in the LORD's sovereign plan for Samuel's life. She knew that she was entrusting her son to One with a beautiful plan. In her surrender of control, she recognized that she, along with everyone else, was subject to the Sovereignty of the LORD of Hosts.

Since their family's custom was to travel to the temple once a year, Hannah was entrusting the LORD and the LORD's chosen priest, Eli, with the life of her child. She was giving up her job as mother in order that Samuel could be used by the LORD of Hosts for His kingdom purposes. Because she upheld the LORD as having authority over all the hosts of heaven and earth, she considered Him worthy of her child. Secondly, a son would provide security and provision for Hannah should she become a widow throughout her life. Not only did Hannah place her child's life in the capable hands of the LORD, but she gave up her culture's means of provision and security. This act evidenced her faith in the LORD of Hosts to command and carry out her provision and security. Hannah believed that His ability was immeasurably greater than any human means of provision and security. Because Hannah considered the all-powerful, LORD of Hosts worthy of her thankfulness and trust, Hannah did not cling to her gift but gave Samuel back to God. She did not know it at the time, but Hannah would be blessed with a total of six children throughout her lifetime.

We might expect great sorrow from Hannah as she left her young boy with Eli in the house of the LORD at Shiloh, but her prayer immediately after fulfilling her vow to dedicate Samuel to the LORD for all of the days of his life was filled with praise! Remember, Hannah had called upon YHWH Sabaoth in her time of distress. She called upon the One who had power and authority over all the hosts and armies of heaven and earth. She began and ended her prayer with declarations that it is the LORD that exalts. Hannah attributed all strength as coming from and belonging to the LORD in stating "there is no rock like our God" (1 Sam. 2:2). Additionally, Hannah recognized that the LORD breaks the bows of the mighty/proud but gives strength to the feeble (1 Sam. 2:4). Clearly, Hannah knew that she was weak and unable to provide for herself, yet the LORD of Hosts was mighty and able. She praised the LORD of Hosts for His provision in providing food, children, and life (1 Sam. 2:5-6). Throughout her prayer, Hannah recognized the unchanging, never-ending identity of the LORD: He is YHWH Sabaoth.

Hannah's testimony should encourage us to attribute all authority and power to YHWH Sabaoth. He is in control of times and seasons. He raises up and tears down according to His Sovereign purposes. In what ways do you need to surrender to the command and authority of the LORD of Hosts? In what areas of your life do you need His victory? As Hannah did, cry out to the LORD of Hosts! He hears the cries of His faithful ones. He defends the cause of the weak and humble.

WEDNESDAY AND THURSDAY (DAY 3 AND 4): DAVID AND THE LORD OF HOSTS

Over the next two days, we will be studying select passages in which David refers to the LORD God as "the LORD of Hosts." In the first selection of Scripture, David faced Goliath in battle. Prior to this passage, the first king of Israel, Saul, had been rejected by the LORD due to his disregard of the LORD's commands. While Saul was still king, the LORD sent the prophet, Samuel, to anoint the next king. David was chosen by YHWH Sabaoth as the next king of Israel. David was so unlikely a choice for king, that his own father did not even call him in from tending to the sheep to be considered as king. He was youngest in his family, but "the LORD sees not as man sees: man looks on the outward appearance, but the LORD looks on the heart" (1 Sam. 16:7). After being privately anointed as king and being rushed upon by the Spirit (1 Sam. 16:13), David was asked to serve King Saul by playing the harp for him whenever he was inflicted with a harmful spirit. When David wasn't serving King Saul, he traveled home to continue the lowly work of a shepherd for his father.

After some time passed, the Philistines gathered their armies for war against the Israelites. While the two armies gathered and encamped in preparation for battle, the Philistines' champion named Goliath of Gath pridefully demanded day after day that the Israelites choose a man to come and fight against him. David's oldest three brothers were serving in Israel's army; therefore, David was sent by his father to bring them food. David witnessed Goliath's haughty words that defied the armies of the living God. He witnessed the men of Israel's great fear of Goliath. "David said to Saul, 'Let no man's heart fail because of him. Your servant will go and fight with the Philistine'" (1 Sam. 17:32). David knew, for the Spirit of the living God was upon him, and that the LORD of Hosts would deliver the Philistines into their hands. "For the battle is the LORD's" (1 Sam. 18:47).

After leading the Israelites in victory against the Philistines, David's life became riddled with trials. Saul became jealous of David; therefore, David was forced to flee for his life. He was forced to live life as an outlaw and endure assassination attempts at the command of Saul. Although David experienced much suffering, he was also given great victories by the LORD of Hosts. By the power of God Almighty, He became a hero in Saul's army, King of Judah, and King of Israel. He conquered Jerusalem and brought the Ark of the Covenant into Jerusalem. The second two passages that will be studied over the next two days land directly after David brings the "Ark of Covenant, which is called by the name of the LORD of Hosts who sits enthroned on the cherubim" into Jerusalem (2 Sam. 6:2). As YHWH Sabaoth reigned in David's life, David reigned over all of Israel in His strength. After being anointed king of Israel and taking Jerusalem back for the people of Israel, it is said that "David became greater and greater, for the LORD of Hosts was with him" (1 Chron. 11:9).

Through both trials and victories, David loved the LORD and desired to create a house for the LORD to dwell. The LORD of Hosts spoke to David through Nathan the prophet, and David's response was one of humility and praise to the LORD of Hosts who is God over all. The LORD of Hosts, YHWH Sabaoth, is in control of all the forces of Heaven and earth, and He alone receives the credit for David's great accomplishments. At the same time, the hardships that David endured were equally ordained by the LORD of Hosts for David's ultimate good. As we study YHWH Sabaoth, we must learn to recognize the truth that all the times are in His hands both pleasant and unpleasant. The LORD does not waste suffering; rather, He uses trials as a means of accomplishing the eternal, inner work of molding a person into His image. As you study, consider how YHWH Sabaoth reveals Himself through the events in David's life and David's response to the God of all the hosts of heaven and earth. How might YHWH Sabaoth want you to recognize Him and praise Him for His work in your life?

READ 1 SAMUEL 17:38-54.
Why do you think the Philistine (Goliath) disdained David?

In your own words, what insults did the Philistine (Goliath) hurl at David?

Using verse 45, what is the contrast between the weapons of the Philistine and David?

What did David prophesy would occur in verse 46? How do you think that this made the Philistine feel?

What was God's purpose behind the events between the Israelites and Philistines and David and Goliath?

In what specific ways was David's prophesy fulfilled?

READ 2 SAMUEL 7:1-17.
What was the desire of David's heart? What do you think fueled this desire?

The LORD referred to Himself as "the LORD of Hosts" in verse 8. How do you think His name relates to the work that He had already done in David's life? (Focus on verses 8-9a.).

Briefly list several future-promise statements that YHWH Sabaoth makes to David.

How do you think the LORD of Hosts' character as the all-powerful, completely sovereign, God over all the armies of earth and Heaven will be displayed through His future plans?

READ 2 SAMUEL 7:18-29.
Using verses 18-19, how does David respond to the LORD of Hosts' covenant to himself? What attitude does he seem to have toward the LORD?

In verse 21, what reason does David give for the LORD bringing greatness to David?

For what does David praise the Lord God in verses 22-24?

Note: In verse 26, David declares that the name of the LORD, the LORD of Hosts, will be magnified forever because He is God over Israel and because the house of David will be established forever.

Why do you think David connects "the LORD of Hosts" with the acts of God being over Israel and the establishment of the house of David?

Through these passages, it is clear that David had faith in the LORD as ruler over all the hosts and armies of the universe. He believed that He was LORD of war and the outcomes of war. YHWH Sabaoth is all-powerful, all-knowing, and completely sovereign over all the workings of the earth and David stood on these truths as He fearlessly faced Goliath in the name of the LORD of Hosts. He knew that any weapon or warrior that stood against YHWH Sabaoth would be brought low by the All-Powerful. In giving David the victory, all who were gathered learned that "there is a God in Israel" and that "the LORD saves not with sword and spear" (1 Sam. 17:46-47). In the same way, the children of God do not have to tremble in the face of terrifying circumstances, yet they can carry out the will of the LORD of Hosts knowing that He wills and works all things for His glory and wonderful purposes. When the people of God are chosen to be a part of the work of the LORD their only response is that of glorifying the One who gives victory.

In 2 Samuel 7, we found that David longed to build a house for the LORD. In response to David's desire, the LORD spoke to David through the prophet, Nathan. YHWH tells David that He had not commanded David to build Him a house. The LORD called Himself "the LORD of Hosts" and reminded David that He exalted David from His lowly position as shepherd and made him a prince over His people, Israel (2 Sam. 7:8). The LORD of Hosts alone has the power to make one's name great, to give victory over enemies, to plant nations and uproot them, to grant peace, to raise up offspring, to establish kingdoms, and to establish thrones forever. David's response to YHWH Sabaoth's work in his life was: "Who am I, O Lord God, and what is my house, that you have brought me thus far" (2 Sam. 7:18)? David gives all acclaim to the LORD for his success and makes it known that he finds himself unworthy of all of the blessings bestowed upon him. As if the success that the LORD of Hosts had already brought into David's life was not enough, the LORD of Hosts made a Covenant with David promising to build David a house in which he would experience peace from his enemies. The LORD stated that he would establish David's kingdom through His offspring, Solomon. "Your house and your kingdom shall be made sure forever before me. Your throne shall be established forever" (2 Sam. 7:16). We find the fulfillment of this promise in Jesus Christ, the Messiah, who came through the line of David.

After a long list of David's victories, in 2 Samuel 8:14 we found that "the LORD gave victory to David wherever he went. As the great LORD of Hosts administered justice and equity to His people, David was enabled by the Mighty One to do the same (2 Sam. 8:15). We learn from these passages that all success is given to us by the LORD of Hosts. He alone is the author of victory; therefore, He deserves all of the glory. "Who is this King of glory? The LORD of hosts, he is the King of glory"

(Ps. 24:10)! As David responded to the LORD of Hosts, ask Him today, "Who am I, O Lord GOD, and what is my house, that you have brought me thus far?" and recognize that all of the mighty things that the LORD of Hosts has worked in your life are "small things in [His] eyes" (2 Sam. 7:18-19). The LORD of Hosts is great and worthy of all glory! As you recognize success in your life, remember to attribute such success to the One truly responsible.

FRIDAY (DAY 5): REFLECTION

As you reflect upon the past week of Bible study, prayerfully and honestly answer the following questions.

In what areas of your life do you need to call upon the LORD of Hosts?

What accomplishments and successes have you knowingly or unknowingly taken the credit for? Make a list and take time to glorify the LORD of Hosts for each victory granted in your life.

Write a prayer of submission to the LORD's authority, timing, and control. Praise Him for being the one capable of bringing victory in your life for His glory.

MONDAY AND TUESDAY (DAY 6 AND 7): THE LORD OF HOSTS' JUDGMENT AGAINST THE WICKED

As we have studied YHWH Sabaoth in the context of Hannah and David's lives, we have focused on mighty things that the Commander of all of the armies of heaven of earth can and will do on behalf of His chosen people. While it is tempting to skip over the aspects of YHWH Sabaoth that make us uncomfortable, we must recognize that as the LORD of Hosts wields victory for His people, He is, at the same time wielding judgment against His enemies. As the LORD of Hosts gave David victory, He orchestrated the judgment of the wicked Philistines. The LORD of Hosts brings forth righteous judgment against wickedness and sin and promises that sin will not go unpunished for He is just in all of His ways. The same God who is all-together omnipotent and sovereign, who is in control of the hosts of heaven and earth, will carry out judgment against wickedness.

In the passages we will study throughout the next two days, we will learn of the LORD of Hosts" judgment against evil. After urging Israel to repent of their evil deeds, the LORD of Hosts warns of a day in Isaiah's time in which He would reject those that continued in their pride, idolatry, greed, and overall wickedness despite the LORD's rebukes through His prophet, Isaiah. Isaiah was prophesying judgment at the hand of the LORD of Hosts because the LORD alone should be exalted, and man considered of no account when compared to His majesty. To call upon YHWH Sabaoth is to realize how mighty He is, having all things at His command. Who are we, His creation, to defy His holy standards with pride and self-idolatry?

After studying passages in Isaiah, we will study the return of Jesus Christ to the earth as the hosts of heaven and the Bride of Christ, return to the earth for a great battle against Satan, the antichrist, false prophet, earth's wicked kings and all who have followed them to make war against the King of kings and Lord of lords. In Revelation 19, we find that Jesus returns in total righteousness as He judges and makes war against the armies of Satan. He is completely victorious as the wicked suffer at the hand of the Almighty. As you study YHWH Sabaoth, remember that He, the LORD of Hosts, has purposed to deal with us according to our ways and deeds (Zech. 1:6), yet made a way for men and women to be saved from His wrath. This should invoke within us a healthy fear and reverence for the all-powerful LORD of Hosts. "The fear of the LORD is the beginning of wisdom, and the knowledge of the Holy One is insight" (Prov. 9:10).

The truths mentioned above should also comfort our hearts. Maybe you or someone you love has experienced abuse or violence at the hands of another. Maybe it seems like justice hasn't been accomplished. The LORD of Hosts says, "Beloved, never avenge yourselves, but leave it to the wrath of God, for it is written, 'vengeance is mine, I will repay, says the Lord'" (Rom. 12:19). A Christian doesn't have to worry about a lack of justice on the earth. There will come a day in which each person will stand before the LORD of Hosts and give an account for their actions. As we recognize that vengeance belongs to the LORD, Christians are freed up to love their enemies, do good to those that hurt them, bless those that curse them, and pray for those that abuse them (Luke 18:8). Ask the LORD to humble you under His mighty power as you submit to His leadership and follow Him in accordance with His commands.

READ ISAIAH 2:6-10.
What reasons are given for the LORD rejecting people?

In what ways, if any, are you tempted to bow down to the work of your hands?

Using verse 10, write three adjectives that describe the LORD.

READ ISAIAH 2:11-22.
Who does the LORD of Hosts have a day against?

How many times does Isaiah refer to God's opposition to prideful mankind in this passage?

Why do you think the LORD of Hosts opposes anyone and anything that exalts itself against Him? (See also, Isa. 30:18.)

Rewrite the command in verse 22 in your own words.

READ REVELATION 19:11-16.
Describe the One riding on the white horse using verses 11-13.

Who was following Jesus? (See also, Rev. 19:7-9.)

Describe the contrast of the portrayal of Jesus in verses 15-16 and Isaiah 53:3-7.

Why is Jesus worthy to carry out God's wrath against wickedness? (See also, Rev. 5:9-10.)

READ REVELATION 19:17-21.
Who had gathered against the LORD of Hosts?

What was the outcome of those that made war against "him who was sitting on the horse and against his army" (Rev. 19:19)?

READ PSALM 145:17 AND PSALM 7:11.
How do these verses describe the ways and character of the LORD?

"Holy, holy, holy, is the LORD of Hosts, the whole earth is full of His glory" (Isa. 6:3), and yet we have all committed high treason against Him as we have defied His commands and loved our sin. Isaiah 2 and Revelation 19 both paint a terrifying picture of the wrath of God being carried out by the LORD of Hosts — wrath that we all rightly deserve. Isaiah writes, "enter the caverns of the rocks and the clefts of the cliffs, from before the terror of the LORD, and from the splendor of his majesty when he rises to terrify the earth" (Isa. 2:20-21). There is no force powerful enough to combat His just wrath when the time comes. In the final battle, not even Satan and his armies will stand a chance against the LORD of Hosts as Jesus "treads the winepress of the fury of the wrath of God the Almighty" (Rev. 19:15). After studying these Scriptures, our hearts long to be on the LORD of Hosts' side.

We studied in Revelation 19:14, that the King of kings and Lord of lords will be followed by the armies of heaven who have been arrayed in fine linen, white and pure which stands for the righteous deeds of the saints (Rev. 19:8). The spotless Lamb of God, Jesus, bore the just punishment, the terrifying wrath of God Almighty, for our sins so that we might become the righteousness of Christ (2 Cor. 5:21). It is through the slain Lamb's atoning sacrifice, that the Bride of Christ is justified and made clean. The Bride is counted righteous by grace through faith and shares in the victory of Jesus Christ as He wages war against Satan's army. The people belonging to the LORD of Hosts follow Jesus as he carries out justice (Rev. 19:14). "When justice is done, it is a joy to the righteous but terror to the evildoers" (Prov. 21:15). Today, if you are in Christ and have been redeemed by the blood of the slain Lamb, praise Him for your salvation! His Salvation provided to you through Jesus makes the LORD of Hosts for you and not against you. Because of Jesus, you are able to rest knowing that you are and will be on the winning side of history. Praise the LORD of Hosts for His awesome, unstoppable power! Worship Him today!

WEDNESDAY AND THURSDAY (DAY 8 AND 9): THE LORD OF HOSTS ON OUR SIDE

After focusing on the terrifying truths regarding the vengeance of the LORD of Hosts against the wicked and His unstoppable power to bring about defeat to the proud who reject Jesus and refuse to follow Him, we will focus on how the LORD of Hosts takes care of His people for His glory. His wrath against His enemies is unstoppable, but His love for His followers is boundless. The LORD of Hosts is defender of the righteous oppressed, mistreated, and the poor. He hears the cries of His people against all injustice. In Zechariah 10:3 the LORD of Hosts is said to "care for his flock." As The LORD of Heaven's Armies cares for His little sheep, the righteous followers, He Himself is their strength. The people of God "have strength through the LORD of hosts, their God" (Zech. 12:5). If you are in Christ, you have the care, strength, and protection of the LORD of Hosts.

Those that exhibit fear of the LORD, believe in Him, and follow Him as the Sovereign One are able to relish in His enduring love for eternity. The enjoyment of His benefits begins on earth. As we face distressing circumstances, the LORD's people are able to call upon Him for aide. The LORD is infinitely on the side of those that belong to Himself. He answers, sets free, and helps His people to the point in which they can look in triumph upon their circumstances and declare "The LORD is on my side; I will not fear. What can man do to me" (Ps. 118:6)? Because of YHWH's nature as Sabaoth, the people of God can take refuge in Him and find that He is their strength, song, and salvation. As you study more passages regarding YHWH Sabaoth, ask the LORD to remind you that, "the LORD is a man of war; the LORD is his name" (Exod. 15:3) and "the LORD will fight for you, and you have only to be silent" (Exodus 14:14). The same LORD who is a man of war, fights for and defends the cause of His flock with great care. Remember, you are not left defenseless to flounder through life, the LORD of Hosts' nature is to come to you in your hour of need. Take an honest look at your heart. Do you truly believe that YHWH is on your side, or have you listened the accuser's, Satan's, lies about the character of the LORD for too long? Who or what you turn to in hardship will reveal to you who or what is on the throne in the LORD of Hosts' rightful place in your life.

READ JAMES 5:1-6.

What were the accusations against the wicked rich?

Who is crying out against the injustice?

Whose ears do the cries reach?

How might the cries reaching the LORD of Hosts ears comfort the mistreated?

How might the idea of the LORD of the armies of heaven and earth terrify the ones that stand condemned before the Almighty?

READ JAMES 5:7-12.
How does focusing on the coming of the Lord help His people to be patient?

What do you think that it means to "establish your hearts" knowing that the coming of the LORD is at hand?

Why might affirming the truth that "the Judge is standing at the door," encourage believers to walk in righteousness and obey the commands of the LORD?

Keeping in mind the character of the LORD of Hosts as the commander of all things, explain how Christians are able to be patient in the midst of suffering?

READ PSALM 118:4-9.
Special Note: The word for "fear" in verse 4 is the Hebrew verb "yare" which can me to fear, revere, or stand in awe.

In your own words, what do you think that it means to "fear the LORD?" (See also, Prov. 1:7, 8:13, Job 28:28, Ecc. 12:13)

How does the LORD respond when His servant is in distress?

What truths can you cling to within
these verses when you feel afraid?

What does it mean that "the LORD is on my side?"
(See also, Rom. 8:30-32, Prov. 3:26, 2 Tim. 4:17-18.)

Christians can expect suffering and mistreatment at the hands of the wicked. Christians can expect to endure spiritual warfare against the forces of darkness. Christians are not exempt from the effects of living in a sin-stricken, fallen world: death, sickness, and loss. Job was described by God as "a blameless and upright man, who fears God and turns away from evil" (Job 1:9), and yet He suffered the loss of property, children, and his health. James uses Job as an example of steadfastness in the midst of suffering. He remarked on the LORD's purpose in allowing Job's suffering as being founded in compassion and mercy. The ones who remain steadfast in the midst of oppression and trials are declared as blessed. They are blessed because God is working within them His good purposes — the purpose of conforming His children into the image of Jesus (Rom. 8:28-29). They are able to be patient and establish their hearts because of the truth that the Lord is coming back, and He will bring restoration. All of the wrong things in the world will be made right again when Jesus returns. As we look to the return of Christ, remember Jesus' words " I am coming soon. Hold fast what you have, so that no one may seize your crown" (Rev. 3:11). Do not give up; rather, look to and love the return of Jesus as you grow weary. Remember, "there is laid up for [Christians] the crown of righteousness, which the Lord, the righteous judge, will award to me on that Day, and not only to me but also to all who have loved his appearing" (2 Tim. 4:8).

The coming King is also the judge with the power to carry out His right judgments as the LORD of Hosts; therefore, it is encouraging for Christians to know that the LORD of Hosts is for them and concerned about their good. Just as YHWH Sabaoth is sovereign over the armies of Heaven and Earth, He is sovereign over the suffering and victories in our lives. As His plan unfolds, Christians rest in the truths that He cares deeply (1 Pet. 5:7), will meet their needs (Phil. 4:19), and is always right beside them (Acts. 2:25). He stands by His people and gives them strength to press on. Although one might be asked to endure oppression at the hand of the wicked, the cries for justice have certainly reached the LORD of Hosts who will carry out judgment upon those that stand in opposition to Himself and His people. The coming judge, YHWH Sabaoth, cares deeply about the suffering of His people. He will respond. He will return. He will bring healing to His people. He will reward those that have suffered in patience knowing that He is in charge of all, and nothing escapes His mighty command.

Are you suffering today? If so, replace your anxious, hurt thoughts with truths about the coming King and the reward of eternal life for all who believe. If you are being mistreated or oppressed, remember Christ also suffered while on earth. In fact, He suffered for us. He is our example, and we must follow Him. "When He was reviled, He did not revile in return; when He suffered, He did not threaten, but continued entrusting Himself to Him who judges justly" (1 Pet. 2:21-23). The Judge, the LORD of Hosts, will return to the earth and defend His people. Today, ask the LORD to help you pray alongside the martyrs mentioned in Revelation 6: "O Sovereign Lord, holy and true, how long before you will judge and avenge our blood …" (Rev. 6:10). Let "the Spirit and the Bride say, 'come,' And let the one who hears say, 'come'" (Rev. 22:17) as we look to and long for the justice and leadership of Jesus on the earth.

FRIDAY (DAY 10): REFLECTION

After this past week of Bible study, prayerfully and thoughtfully respond to the following reflection questions.

How would you describe your response to
learning about YHWH Sabaoth's wrath
and judgments against wickedness?

In what ways do you find comfort in the attributes
of YHWH Sabaoth? Write a prayer of thanksgiving.

In what ways does looking to the return of Christ
strengthen your heart to endure suffering on the earth?

LESSON 7: YHWH TSIDKENU, THE LORD OUR RIGHTEOUSNESS

Throughout the next two weeks, we will be studying another compound name by which the LORD is called, YHWH Tsidkenu. The word "tsidkenu" is translated as "our righteousness." The first time the LORD is referred to as the LORD Our Righteousness lands in Jeremiah 23. The second time is in Jeremiah 33. Jeremiah became a prophet during King Josiah's reign. King Josiah was the last faithful king in Judah's history. After Josiah's death, Judah spiraled downward and away from the one, true God. They were altogether unrighteous. Due to their adulterous behavior against the LORD, Judah endured troubled times that led to their demise politically, socially, financially, and spiritually. Judah suffered from Egyptian political dominance, Babylonian captivity, and invasion. Their decline lasted for 20 years before Judah ceased to be a nation. Although Jeremiah did not see the complete demise of Judah, he became a prophet to the nations (Jer. 1:5) by preaching against the sins of Judah, Egypt, Babylon, and other associated countries throughout their trouble.

Jeremiah bore witness to multiple transfers of Judean captives to Babylon, the destruction of Jerusalem, and the destruction of the temple. Jeremiah faithfully declared the Word of the LORD and put the blame of Jerusalem's fall and sufferings directly upon Judah due to their unfaithfulness and refusal to stop listening to false prophets. It is in the midst of these tumultuous times that a key theme emerges within the book of Jeremiah — a Messiah was coming. Jeremiah prophesies a time in which God would raise up a king for the faithful remnant in Israel to reign over them. This king is referred to as "a righteous Branch" and is prophesied to be their righteousness. After experiencing life with faithful King Josiah and then enduring faithless kings, Jeremiah must have longed for the LORD's promise to send a king to be the peoples' righteousness — a king from the line of David. Over 100 times, Jeremiah urged God's people to repent. Jeremiah exhibited faith that the LORD would heal a repentant people, but the people did not repent. Jeremiah mourned and wept over their lack of repentance and is often referred to as the "weeping prophet." Jeremiah was comforted by the LORD as He revealed to Jeremiah that He promised to raise up the righteous Branch that would be called, "The LORD Our Righteousness." Renewal would eventually come. The repentant would one day be counted righteous! He is YHWH Tsidkenu!

When Tsidkenu is attached to the LORD's name, the word describes an aspect of His unfailing and unchanging character. He was, is, and always will be the LORD Our Righteousness. He is Our Righteousness because that is His identity, and YHWH never changes. Since it is true that the LORD is Our Righteous, who is the "our?" Who is it that benefits from His righteousness since He is "Our Righteousness?" Truly, all have sinned and fallen short of the glory of God (Rom. 3:23). The only hope we have of being counted as righteous in the sight of God is a righteousness outside of ourselves. The LORD imputes His righteousness and completely justifies anyone as a gift by His grace through faith in Jesus Christ's sacrifice for sins in dying on the cross. When we consider the LORD's imputed righteousness upon a believer, we understand that the LORD Our Righteousness represents us as righteous when we stand before God Almighty to receive judgment for our sins against God. It is the righteousness of God alone that saves us from eternal damnation in hell. Once we receive salvation by grace through faith in Christ alone, He will always stand as Our Righteousness in the presence of God as He makes intercession on our behalf (Heb. 7:25). If He is Our Righteousness, He is able to keep our righteousness intact before the Holy One as we continually fall short of God's standard. Because of YHWH Tsidkenu, the LORD Our Righteousness, we have a righteousness that is not based upon our actions but on Christ's actions. As you study YHWH Tsidkenu this week, continually consider that His righteousness is the only hope we have of obtaining right standing with God. Remember, since "Our Righteousness" is an aspect of His identity, it can be counted upon for Salvation.

MONDAY AND TUESDAY (DAY 1 AND 2): BUILDING CONTEXT

Christians are sometimes accused of being "self-righteous" and "holier-than-thou" by people because Christians refuse to participate in behaviors that the LORD condemns. Has this happened to you? Of course, some professing Christians might have developed a pharisee-type mindset in which they truly do look down upon other people, consider themselves as holier than others, and/or trust in their legalistic rule-following and good works for their self-granted status as "righteousness." The last thing a Christian should want is to give off the impression that their "good works" and "self-righteousness" will save them. The Bible teaches the opposite: "For by grace you have been saved through faith. And this is not your own doing; it is a gift of God, not a result of works, so that no one may boast" (Eph. 2:8-9). A true Christian will boldly proclaim that the only hope a person has in being counted as righteous in the sight of YHWH is faith in Jesus Christ — Our Righteousness.

Over the next two days, we will focus on the first passage, Jeremiah 23:1-6, in which the LORD is named "The LORD Our Righteousness". In this passage of Scripture, the sheep/flock are widely considered to be God's people: Judah. Judah is mentioned specifically in the passage today; therefore, it is important to know that Judah is a tribe of Israel — a part of the whole. Judah is the tribe through which the Messiah was prophesied to come; therefore, Jesus is from the tribe of Judah. In Revelation 5:5, Jesus is called "the Lion of the tribe of Judah, the root of David." The phrase, "root of David," can be explained by the fact that Jesus' genealogy on both his earthly father's and mother's side led back to David.

YHWH promised the coming son of David hundreds of years before Jesus was born to Mary and Joseph. This is a reminder to YHWH's followers that He has had a plan from the foundation of the world to make those in Christ holy and without blame before Himself (Eph. 1:4). In a historical period in which spiritual leaders, kings, Israelites, and pagan nations acted wickedly, Jeremiah prophesied that the LORD would raise up a "righteous Branch" that would "reign as king." In the days of this "righteous Branch," God's people would call YHWH, the LORD Our Righteousness. This "righteous Branch" is none other than Jesus, who is our righteousness, sanctification, and redemption (1 Cor. 1:30). The shepherds in this passage represent those who God had given His people as leaders, specifically the kings that reigned in Judah. In this passage, we will find that while all human leaders fail, the LORD is committed to care for those that He predestined to be adopted as sons in daughters.

As you study this prophesy, allow the LORD to build faith in your heart. You must have faith in His righteousness, rather than a misplaced faith in the possibility of earning the status of "righteous" by your own actions. If you feel as though you could never be counted righteous in God's sight, remember that He has not abandoned you due to your sins. He is righteous enough to pursue after each person belonging to Himself despite their unrighteous actions because He Himself is their righteousness by nature. Today, as you read, ask YHWH Tsidkenu to reveal Himself to you as the Righteous Branch through the study of His Word. Meditate upon the truth that it was completely for the sake of God's people that YHWH made Jesus to be sin, though He was perfect, so that we might become the very righteousness of God (2 Cor. 5:21).

READ JEREMIAH 23:1-4.
What were the shepherds supposed to be doing for the flock? (See also, Jer. 3:15.)

How had the shepherds treated the sheep?

How did the LORD respond to the actions of the shepherds?

READ LUKE 15:1-7 ALONGSIDE JEREMIAH 23:4.
What is the spiritual state of a person (sheep) that is either missing or lost?

How would you expect the LORD Our Righteousness to respond to a sinful person that has gone astray from the flock?

When a sheep/person goes missing, how does the LORD respond?

What does this reveal about the LORD's care over His flock?

What emotions does the shepherd display in regard to His sheep?

READ JEREMIAH 23:5-6 AND ISAIAH 11:1-5.
What will the LORD raise up?

Using the following verses, Matthew 2:2, Luke 1:32, Luke 19:38, John 1:49, who was the King, the Branch, the Messiah that the Israelites were expecting?

What is the character of the Branch?

How does the raising up of the "Branch" honor God's covenant to David from 2 Samuel 7:16-17?

Based on Jeremiah 23:5 and Zechariah 6:12-13, how might the Israelites have expected the Branch (the Messiah) to come?

The LORD said that He would raise up "for David a righteous Branch" that would "reign as king and deal wisely, and [would] execute justice and righteousness in the land"(Jer. 23:5). The fact that God stated that the coming Branch, the Messiah, the King of Kings would come from David's line "for David" is astounding. Jesus did in fact come through David's genealogy. Jesus was sent for David, but He was not just sent for David. "Christ Jesus came into the world to save sinners" (1 Tim. 1:15) so that "whoever believes in Him shall not perish, but have eternal life" (John 3:16). In 2 Samuel 7, the LORD of Hosts made David a promise that his "kingdom shall be made sure forever … (2 Sam. 7:16). The LORD made David's kingdom "sure forever" by placing the eternal, self-existent King of kings inside a young girl from David's line's womb. Not only can the LORD's words be completely trusted due to His promise-keeping nature, but the fulfillment of prophesy from hundreds of years prior to Jesus' incarnation reveals God's omniscience and sovereignty over everything that happens on the earth.

The Branch to come was one that the Jews believed would reign and deliver them from the oppression of Roman rule. The Jews were expecting a conquering king as they read or listened to these passages in Jeremiah, yet Jesus came to execute justice and righteousness in the land in an unexpected fashion. After Jesus performed the miracle in which he fed 5,000 men, Jesus perceived that the crowd was going to take Him by force and make Him king; therefore, He slipped away (John 6:15). The people longed for freedom from the Romans, yet Jesus' kingship during His first trip to earth was a spiritual kingship. As Jesus was questioned by Pilate, the governor of Judea, before His crucifixion, Pilate asked "Are you the King of the Jews" (John 18:33)? Jesus answered, "My kingdom is not of this world" (John 18:36). He was King, and as King, He had come to execute justice and righteousness. He executed justice by taking the just punishment for the wickedness of the entire world. He executed righteousness by making a way for men and women to enter into the status of right standing with God. Today, we must believe these truths about YHWH, and it will be counted to us as righteousness (Rom. 4:3). Do you find yourself striving and working to earn your right standing with YHWH? Are you exhausted by your constant inability to measure up? Remember, there is One who can deliver you. His name is Jesus Christ

— YHWH Tsidkenu. Because He is Our Righteousness, you are no longer condemned (Rom. 8:1). That truth in and of itself makes YHWH worthy of your entire life.

WEDNESDAY AND THURSDAY (DAY 3 AND 4): THE RIGHTEOUS BRANCH

In Jeremiah 23, the LORD is called "the LORD Our Righteousness." In this same passage, the righteous Branch who would reign as king was prophesied. The righteous Branch referred to throughout the Old Testament was known by the Jews to be their long-awaited Messiah. As stated earlier, the Jews were waiting for the one who would "execute justice and righteousness in the land." They believed that the one coming would bring about their physical peace by delivering them out of Roman rule and establishing them as a nation once again. They longed for political freedom from Roman's tyranny. As Jesus' fame spread throughout the surrounding towns, many believed that He was the long-awaited Messiah. Many, particularly the religious leaders and Roman officials, felt threatened by His presence among the people. The leaders were acquainted with Jesus' popularity with both Jewish and Gentile crowds due to His miracles and teachings. A large number of people had become so convinced that Jesus was the answer to their prayers and the end to their waiting, they gave Jesus a kingly welcome as He entered Jerusalem in what is commonly referred to today as the Triumphal Entry. They laid down their clothes and waved palm branches shouting, "Blessed is the King who comes in the name of the Lord" (Luke 19:38)!

Throughout the next two days, look for misconceptions that the Jews held in regard to the Branch, their Messiah. Secondly, ask YHWH Tsidkenu to reveal to you how He brought about righteousness and revealed Himself as Savior in a way contrary to the Jews' expectations. It is beneficial to recognize that we are prone to place expectations on YHWH and interpret Scripture wrongly too. We must actively and humbly search the Scriptures and submit to the LORD's will. Finally, recognize that we too are prone to hope in political deliverance and leaders rather than the plan of YHWH. We are prone to slander and dishonor political leaders that we feel treat us unfairly. According to the Apostle Paul, inspired by the Holy Spirit, we are to "be subject to the governing authorities" because "there is no authority except from God, and those that exist have been instituted by God" (Rom. 13:1). Today, ask the LORD to give you spiritual eyes to see His Kingdom purposes and not become distracted by earthly kingdoms. Ask YHWH to help you avoid the temptation to build your own kingdom based upon your own expectations; rather, submit to the LORD as Jesus taught us to pray: "Your kingdom come, Your will be done, on earth as it is in Heaven (Matt 6:10).

READ MATTHEW 21:1-11.
Special Note: Matthew 21:5 is a quote from Zechariah 9:9.

In your own words, what prophesy is the Lord fulfilling in entering Jerusalem riding on a donkey's colt?

Why do you think Jesus chose to enter riding on a colt as opposed to an adult donkey or a horse?

What actions do the crowd members perform?

How might those actions point to belief/hope that Jesus is the prophesied Davidic king (the Messiah, the Branch) that they had been waiting for to bring salvation? (See also, 2 Kings 9:13.)

What was the crowd shouting?

Special Note: Hosanna means "O save" in Hebrew.

In what ways did Jesus answer the crowds' cries: "O save!" (See also, Matt. 1:21, John 3:16-17, and Rom. 6:23.)

How was Jesus' saving different from what the Jews expected?

How is someone saved? (See also, Eph. 2:8-9.)

How did Jesus' saving work on the cross bring about righteousness? (See also, 2 Cor. 5:21.)

In calling Jesus "Son of David," what is the crowd acknowledging about Jesus? (See also, 2 Sam. 7:12-16.)

How did the city respond to Jesus' entry into Jerusalem?

How did the crowd identify Jesus?

How was Jesus being referred to as "the Prophet" a fulfillment of prophesy? (See also, Deut. 18:15, 18.)

How might a focus on Jesus as "the Prophet" hinder people from seeing Him as their Righteousness — their only hope for being made right with God?

READ 1 PETER 2:22-25.
Describe Jesus' morality and behavior.

Why does this make Him the perfect Lamb to die as our substitutionary atonement? (See also, 1 Pet. 3:18, Exod. 12:5, and 1 Pet. 1:19.)

Explain how verse 24 relates to YHWH Tsidkenu, the LORD Our Righteousness.

How does verse 25 relate to Jeremiah 23:4?

Just before Jesus' Triumphal Entry, Jesus plainly foretold His upcoming death for a third time as He spoke to His twelve disciples. His disciples failed to understand Jesus' plain outline of future events: "The Son of Man will be delivered over to the chief priests and scribes, and they will condemn him to death and deliver him over to the Gentiles to be mocked and flogged and crucified, and he will be raised on the third day" (Matt. 20:18-19). Instead of processing Jesus' words, James and John's mom asked Jesus to give her sons seats on Jesus' right and left side of His throne. This was a conversation that James and John were actively involved in; therefore, whenever the other ten disciples heard about it, they became angry and annoyed. All of the disciples were seeking greatness and recognition, but Jesus taught them that whoever wanted to be great, must become a servant "even as the Son of Man came not to be served but to serve, and to give his life as a ransom for many" (Matt. 20:28). No one, not even Jesus' closest followers, understood the type of righteousness and justice that the Branch would establish.

Although He was King of kings and Messiah, He did not come to the earth to sit on a throne. He did not want His followers seeking thrones and positions of honor. Although He brought about the justice of God, He did not wage war against the political rulers exerting authority over the Jews. YHWH Tsidkenu did in fact execute righteousness in the land, but He did so through death on the cross when he made atonement for sins by His blood. As He entered Jerusalem, He was greeted as the Branch with the national symbol of palm branch waving to hail Jesus as the Davidic king. "The waving of palm branches, which symbolically conveyed the notion of victory over one's enemy, probably indicates that the people mistakenly thought that Jesus would then and there bring national deliverance from Israel's political enemies, the Romans" (ESV Study Bible Commentary, p. 2048).

As the crowd shouted, "Hosanna," meaning "Oh save," they fully expected to be saved from the tyranny of Roman rule, yet Jesus was concerned with the Father's will — to save people from His righteous, just wrath against their sins. YHWH was saving them from Himself and making a way for people to be counted as righteous in His sight. As God's wrath against the sins of the world was poured out on Jesus as He suffered and died on His execution stake, the Perfect One became sin.

Christ became sin so that "in him we might become the righteousness of God" (2 Cor. 5:21). The Branch "bore our sins in his body on the tree, that we might die to sin and live to righteousness" (1 Pet. 2:24). The Davidic righteous Branch executed God's just punishment for sin and brought about righteousness to all who would believe in Jesus as Savior and Lord. "And this is the name by which he will be called: The LORD Our Righteousness" (Jer. 23:6). He's not just "the Branch," "the son of David," or "the Prophet;" Jesus was YHWH in the flesh. And YHWH is the LORD Our Righteousness.

FRIDAY (DAY 5): REFLECTION

Today, thoughtfully and prayerfully answer the following reflection questions.

> What new information did you glean throughout this past week of study that you would like to commit to memory?

> In what ways do you feel led to respond to the LORD Our Righteousness?

In what ways do you see yourself seeking positions and/or honor and need to remember Jesus' words and example: "But whoever wants to be great among you must be your servant" (Matt. 20:26).

MONDAY AND TUESDAY (DAY 6 AND 7): THE RIGHTEOUSNESS OF YHWH TSIDKENU

Throughout the next two days, we will look at passages that describe the righteousness of YHWH Tsidkenu. We will study the connection between Jesus' grace, our righteousness in Him, and eternal life. Completely powerless to answer for our sins against God Almighty and earn right standing with God on our own accord, the One who is perfect in righteousness met the just standard of God for entrance into Heaven. The entire Bible explains that salvation is not found in good works or obedience to the law. No amount of good works approaches the standard for holiness required by the Holy of Holies. The standard for earning Salvation is perfection; therefore, unachievable for humans ruled by a sin nature. Apart from Christ, every human is completely dead in their trespasses and sins (Eph. 2:1). Just as a "No Trespassing" sign is posted as a boundary to tell individuals, "Stop, don't go any further. This is a boundary," the LORD set boundaries for mankind. Every boundary has been ignored and ran past. Our trespasses against God make us spiritual dead outside of Christ. The word "sin" in Ephesians 2:1 comes from the Greek word, hamartano, which means "to miss the mark." The LORD Our Righteousness has expectations and standards for people, yet we have missed the mark and failed to live up to every standard and expectation required for Salvation. Because of our failure to even come close to hitting the mark of holiness, we are dead in sins outside of Christ and completely separated from YHWH. It is because of these truths that we "were by nature children of wrath, like the rest of mankind" (Eph. 2:3).

Despite our trespasses and sins, YHWH had great love, mercy, and kindness for His people (Eph. 2:4). By His own saving power, He made us alive in Christ. He "raised us up with Christ and seated us with him in the heavenly realms in Christ Jesus" (Eph. 2:6). Salvation is only brought about by grace — a free, undeserved gift from YHWH for all who believe. The One Who is Our Righteousness fulfilled all righteousness throughout His life on earth (Matt. 3:15). If being "Our Righteousness" wasn't a part of YHWH's eternal nature, we would be completely ruined. Thankfully, the prophesied "righteous Branch" who was declared by the LORD to reign as king, deal wisely, and execute justice and righteousness in the land shall be called "The LORD Our Righteousness" (Jer. 23:5-6). This week, ask the LORD Our Righteousness to remind you that His righteousness is a free gift. Instead of allowing yourself to question why the LORD is allowing negative things in your life, remember that He gave you the most undeserved, incredible gift: His very own righteousness. Ask YHWH Tsidkenu to grant you a deeper understanding of the Gospel so that you can better articulate it to others.

Describe Jesus' righteousness using the following verses: Hebrews 4:15, Hebrews 7:26, and 1 Peter 2:22.

Read Matthew 3:13-17 and Matthew 5:17 and explain how Jesus' life measured up to God's holy standards.

READ ROMANS 5:12-21.
What do verses 12-14 reveal about the human condition since Adam?

What was the result of Adam's trespass?

What is the "free gift?"

How are humans able to "reign in life?"

What does Jesus' righteousness lead to for all who believe?

According to verse 19, how is one made righteous?

Explain the connection between the LORD's grace, righteousness, eternal life, and Jesus Christ.

READ TITUS 3:5, EPHESIANS 2:8-9, AND GALATIANS 2:16.
What kind of effect do our good works have on our Salvation?

Whose actions secured our Salvation?

Knowing that the LORD is Our Righteousness, how are you prompted to respond? What feelings arise in your heart toward YHWH Tsidkenu?

The righteousness that is ours in Christ has met every standard of God's law — all righteousness was fulfilled in Jesus; therefore, His imputed righteousness upon us because of His blood atonement is able to accomplish for the believer right standing with the LORD. In Romans 5:12-14 we learned that death has reigned from the sin of Adam and Eve on throughout history until present day. Because of sin, both physical and spiritual deaths are realities for all mankind. Just as sin and death were the result of Adam's sin, right standing before the LORD was accomplished for all who believe in Jesus as Savior and give their lives to follow Him as LORD through the finished work of Jesus on the cross.

Jesus' righteousness and obedience to the Father even in death on a cross, brought about the justification and righteousness of believers and granted them the ability to reign in life through Jesus Christ. When we speak of justification in the sight of God, it is as if we have never sinned in the sight of God. Despite our wickedness, we have been granted right standing with God. Justification and righteousness have been given to us as a free gift based upon the life and works of Christ alone. The only way we are able to reign in life in Heaven for all of eternity is through Jesus Christ. May His name be praised forever! We have been given great gifts in Christ that we do not deserve: He has given us His righteousness. His righteousness justifies us before God Almighty as His death answers for our wickedness against God; therefore, we are granted eternal life in Him. The righteousness that belongs to you in Christ is attached to His infinite, unchanging nature; therefore, YHWH Tsidkenu's can be counted upon to be your righteousness. As you trespass and miss the mark, remember that YHWH Tsidkenu's character is to provide you with the righteousness needed to be spared from His wrath. All praise to His great name!

WEDNESDAY AND THURSDAY (DAY 8 AND 9): JESUS CHRIST THE RIGHTEOUSNESS

Over the course of the next two days, we will continue to study passages from the New Testament that explain how Jesus is YHWH Tsidkenu's way through which He accomplishes His name — the LORD Our Righteousness. Jesus is the way through which we receive right standing with God Almighty. We will find that Jesus is referred to in Scripture as, "Jesus Christ the righteousness" in 1 John. Because of Jesus' identity as "the righteousness," those that have come to saving faith will seek to keep His commands. One who has come to YHWH Tsidkenu will love God enough to follow after Him and live a lifestyle that reflects the inner workings of righteousness manifested through obedience to His commands (John 14:15). Although while a person is still on earth, they will wrestle with sin. A true Christian will have a personal relationship with the LORD Our Righteousness that transforms their lifestyles, actions, words, and behaviors in a way that reflects His nature.

Before coming to saving faith in Jesus, men and women would love and choose their sin. Whether we like it or not, the truth is that outside of Jesus' saving work, we were all slaves to sin (John 8:34) and unable to find freedom from patterns of sin without the help of Jesus. After a person admits their sin and repents, they are made new creations by the Holy Spirit (2 Cor. 5:17) and set free from sin, becoming slaves of righteousness (Rom. 6:18). Now, they no longer desire and love their sin. Instead, they hate their sin. Those that love the LORD hate what is evil and hold fast to what is good (Ps. 97:10). It is only through Jesus that a person is able to become free from sin and a slave to righteousness that leads to sanctification (Rom. 6:19).

As you study the Word over the next few days, ask the Holy Spirit to give you an understanding of Jesus' blood atonement for sin and how His propitiation accomplished your righteousness. Jesus' imputed righteousness in the place of our lawlessness in the way through which we find peace with God. The seeking of His righteousness is the way through which we are to battle the temptation to worry about the things of this earth. After commanding His disciples and followers not to worry and become anxious, Jesus tells His people to "seek first the kingdom of God and His righteousness, and all these things (needs such as clothing and food) will be added to you" (Matt. 6:33). Seek first His righteousness today. Seek YHWH Tsidkenu.

READ 1 JOHN 2:1-6.
Christians are encouraged not to sin, but what takes place in heaven when a Christian does sin?

What name is given to Jesus Christ in verse 1?

Use a dictionary and write the definition for the word "propitiation."

How does Jesus' propitiation affect the actions of a Christian?

What does John, the author of 1 John, say of those that express with words their faith but care little for righteous living?

Do you find a connection between the LORD being Our Righteousness and a Christian's desire to keep His commands and live righteously? If so, explain.

Special Note: John gives his readers several ways to test and see if their faith in Jesus the righteousness is genuine throughout 1 John.

READ 1 JOHN 1:7, 2:5, 3:14, 4:13, 5:2.
What types of actions will someone with true faith in Jesus the righteousness exhibit?

What types of actions will someone without true faith in Jesus the righteousness exhibit?

If you were to stand before the LORD Our Righteousness today, how would your faith measure up?

READ ROMANS 3:21-26.
What phrases in this passage suggest that the righteousness of God does not depend on our performance?

Look up a definition for the word "justified." What do you think it means that "we have been justified by his grace as a gift through the redemption that is in Christ Jesus" (vs. 24)?

According to verse 25, what act showed God's righteousness?

How does this "show" of righteousness point to the justice of God? How does it point to Him as the justifier?

According to these verses, at what time is a Christian given the righteousness of God?

According to 1 Corinthians 1:30, what did Jesus Christ become to us?

While Christians seek to please God through obedience to His commands, it is important to keep in mind that our righteousness is never a result of our performance. We are only justified by YHWH Tsidkenu's grace as a gift due to His unending nature. He is our only hope for righteousness before God. If the smallest portion of right standing with God depended upon our righteous acts, we would all be dammed. All are completely powerless to earn righteousness through good works because all have sinned. Our best, most pious moments amount to filthy rags in the sight of the Holy of Holies (Isa. 64:6). Even in Christ, our best moments are often filled with selfishness, evil motives, and evidence of a sinful flesh. Jesus truly is our only hope for righteousness. Christians need to preach the Gospel truths to themselves daily to be reminded of the fact that though they still wrestle with their sinful flesh, Jesus is "Our Righteousness" before our holy God. YHWH Tsidkenu chose not to punish us for our sins but to justify us freely by His grace through Jesus' atonement for our sins. In all things, let us cling to the hope that Jesus Christ has become to us "wisdom from God, righteousness, sanctification, and redemption" (1 Cor. 1:30) to the glory and praise of His great name, YHWH Tsidkenu!

In light of Jesus' great atonement and the knowledge of mankind's powerlessness to become righteous based upon their own merits, Christians' faith in His sacrifice will transfer to the way in which they conduct their lives. Although the Christian will never amount to perfection in performance, their lives will be dedicated to seeking God's will and walking in His ways. On the other hand, if Christians declare to be followers of Christ but set their lives on a path contrary to the LORD's ways and truths, they are exposed as unbelievers. "If we say we have fellowship with him while we walk in darkness, we lie and do not practice the truth. But if we walk in the light, as he is in the light, we have fellowship with one another, and the blood of Jesus his Son cleanses us from all sin" (1 John 1:6-7). What is your attitude toward sin in your life? Is it a pet that you keep with you at all times and enjoy, or is your sin a thorn in your flesh? Jesus declares "If you love me, you will obey my commands" (John 14:15). Only the presence of Christ's saving work in one's life will cause a sinner to hate their sin and love righteousness.

FRIDAY (DAY 10): REFLECTION

Complete the reflection questions below honestly, prayerfully, and faithfully.

Throughout this past week of Bible study, what Scriptures and points stood out to you the most?

How do you know that you having come to saving faith in Jesus' atonement for your sins?

Since YHWH Tsidkenu's nature is closely tied to the Good News of Jesus Christ, how would you explain the Gospel (Good News) to a friend?

Today, take time to write a prayer of praise and thanksgiving to YHWH Tsidkenu for the truths that He highlighted to you as you studied His Word.

LESSON 8: YHWH SHAMMAH, THE LORD IS PRESENT

Over the next two weeks, we will deeply study another name of the LORD- YHWH Shammah. Shammah is translated either as "is present" or "is there;" therefore, YHWH Shammah means "The LORD Is Present" or "The LORD Is There." The LORD was present in a tangible sense, often described as Shekhinah Glory, among His people for much of Israel's history. From the time of Moses and the Exodus from Egypt, God's people had been led by the visible presence of YHWH. His presence was a pillar of cloud by day and a pillar of fire by night (Exod. 13:21). This was the same presence and glory that covered the mountain at Mount Sinai as Moses received the ten commandments of God. Once the Tabernacle, the moving tent of the LORD, was set-up among the Israelites, the presence of the LORD filled the Tabernacle until the time in which King Solomon oversaw the building of God's Holy Temple in the city of Jerusalem. After the construction of the Temple the presence of the LORD was housed within the temple for over 400 years before a dark time in Israel's history in which the LORD's visible manifestation was not present among His people.

Due to Israel's great sin and forsaking of the LORD among them, the glory of the LORD that had been housed within God's Holy Temple after King Solomon brought the Ark of the Covenant into the Holy of Holies (1 Kings 8:1-11) progressively left in Ezekiel 8-11. As Israel's abominations piled up, the LORD withdrew from His people and sent against them judgments in His righteous anger. The temple was destroyed and the holy city, Jerusalem, was defiled. The Jews were carried away into Babylonian captivity to live as exiles. Although Shekhinah Glory was no longer among the Israelites, YHWH Shammah never ceased to be omnipresent. As Jeremiah quotes the voice of the LORD saying: "Can a man hide himself in hiding places so I do not see him … do I not fill the heavens and the earth?" (Jer. 23:24), we understand that the LORD's nature as "present" will never change even when His tangible presence is not discerned. "Is There" or "Is Present" is tied to the LORD's name; therefore, an aspect of His character that cannot be changed by mankind's wicked actions.

Ezekiel was the prophet to which the LORD God spoke to regarding His name for Jerusalem — the LORD Is There. It is clear throughout the book of Ezekiel, that Ezekiel had great concern for the holiness of God and the peoples' sins against the Holy One. While in exile, Ezekiel served the LORD as both prophet and priest to a people who had broken their covenant with the LORD. While Ezekiel's prophecy was written during exceedingly difficult times for God's people, Ezekiel made it clear that these terrible times were brought upon by Judah's faithlessness and adultery against the LORD. As Ezekiel called for repentance, they remained faithless to the LORD. The LORD did not abandon Ezekiel or His chosen people to their despair and hopelessness but spoke beautiful promises in regard to saving His people and restoring their hearts, their city, and His presence to them.

As you study the Scripture surrounding a name in which the LORD ascribed to Himself as He named His holy city, Jerusalem, thank Him for being your ever-present help in the time of need (Ps. 46:1). Remember the words Jesus spoke immediately before ascending into Heaven, "And behold, I am with you always, to the end of the age" (Matt. 28:20).

MONDAY AND TUESDAY (DAY 1 AND 2): JUDGMENT AGAINST JERUSALEM

Over the next two days, we will study passages of Scripture that describe Jerusalem's importance to the LORD, the Israelites' great sins against YHWH, and YHWH Shammah's prophesied judgment against Israel's sin. The LORD Is There's manifest presence had been among His people for generations. His presence was so powerful among them that even the priests could not stand to minister in the house of the LORD because of the awesome glory that filled the Holy of Holies (1 Kings 8:10-11) except on the Day of Atonement after the proper rituals and sacrifices. Although the Shekhinah glory of the LORD among them was a gift and a blessing, the Israelites took YHWH Shammah for granted. Often, the familiar and constant things in our lives are under appreciated. Surely this was the case for the Israelites in regard to the LORD's manifest presence among them.

The LORD had bestowed the blessing of His presence upon His chosen people, yet they rebelled against Him and took Him for granted. Their great sin against the Holy One in their midst resulted in their captivity and the absence of the tangible presence of God among them. As you study this dark period in Israel's history, remember that attaching words to God's personal name is an act of describing His infinite and unchanging character. Even though the glory of the LORD had departed from the midst of Israel, YHWH remained present. Even in Israel's darkest moments, YHWH did not forsake His people. We can take courage in the truth that God's people have been engraved on the palm of His hands (Isa. 49:16). The LORD keeps count of all of our sorrows — even the ones that are self-inflicted. He puts every single one of our tears in a bottle (Ps. 56:8). The LORD cares too much and is too deeply committed to His people for His name's sake to deny His nature as Shammah. Despite feelings, circumstances, and sinful behavior, the people of God can always declare: "Where can I go from Your Spirit? Or where can I flee from Your presence? If I ascend to heaven, You are there; If I make my bed in Sheol, behold, You are there. If I take the wings of the dawn, if I dwell in the remotest part of the sea, even there Your hand will lead me, and Your right hand will lay hold of me" (Ps. 139:7-10). He is YHWH Shammah for all eternity!

READ PSALM 48:1-8.
What are the names ascribed to Jerusalem in these verses?

From these verses, why do you think Jerusalem is important to God?

READ PSALM 132:13-14.
Note: Zion can be symbolic of the kingdom of heaven or represent Jerusalem, the city of David.

What has the LORD chosen?

What reason is given for His choice?

READ EZEKIEL 5:5-12.
According to Ezekiel in verse 5, what position does Jerusalem hold in the eyes of God when compared to the other nations?

In what ways did the people of Jerusalem rebel?

How did Jerusalem's sin compare to that of the surrounding pagan nations?

Due to Jerusalem's rebellion, what was the LORD's response?

List the judgments against the inhabitants of Jerusalem described in these verses due to their wickedness.

How do Ezekiel 5:10 and Lamentations 4:1-2 demonstrate the desperation of the inhabitants of Jerusalem in light of the judgments the people will face?

What reasons does the LORD give for withdrawing His presence (vs. 11)?

Although the LORD withdrew His presence, what remained true about YHWH Shammah? (See also, Ps. 139:7-10, Col. 1:17, Prov. 15:3, Jer. 23:24.)

Although the LORD's presence was within the temple, what further insight does Acts 17:24 provide about His nature?

How do you think the consequences of Israel's sins might be carried out and orchestrated for Israel's eternal good? (See also, 2 Tim. 2:25, Ezek. 18:21-23, Rom. 2:5, Luke 13:3.)

Ezekiel's service to God and Israel as a prophet was entirely from exile. Ezekiel makes it clear that the blame for all of the hardships that fell upon the Israelites rested fully upon the shoulders of God's chosen people. They had been warned, yet they continued to commit idolatry and injustices. Their continual wickedness and disregard for the statues and rules of their God resulted in just punishment. Think about it like this, every abomination performed by God's people was done in the presence of the LORD who had parted the seas on their behalf and delivered them from their troubles time and time again. Solomon spoke to the truth that nothing escapes the notice of YHWH: "The eyes of the LORD are in every place, keeping watch on the evil and the good" (Prov. 15:3). The LORD was present for every action done in darkness by the Israelites, yet He did not strike them down on the spot. If the LORD had rejected the Israelites due to their sin and refused to carry out strong discipline, the Israelites would have certainly continued in their ways, never repented, died in their sins, and experience an eternity away from YHWH Shammah in Hell.

In His holiness and perfect justice, the LORD caused Jerusalem to fall, the temple to be destroyed, and hands His people over to the horrendous effects of siege warfare. Jerusalem would be brought so low that "fathers shall eat their sons" and "sons shall eat their fathers" (Ezek. 5:10). Even worse, the judgment executed upon Israel would include the withdrawing of the Shekhinah glory of the LORD (Ezek. 10). Every judgment Ezekiel prophesied came to pass as Israel was humbled. Despite these historical events, the LORD spoke words of hope to Ezekiel. YHWH Shammah promised that one day, He would place His Spirit within His people so that they might live. He would cause their dry, wicked bones to come to life (Ezek. 37:14). YHWH declared that one day, He would vindicate His holiness, return His people to their land, cleanse them from their sins, give them new hearts, remove their stones of flesh, and cause them to walk in His presence once again (Ezek. 36:23-28). The LORD carried out His strong discipline for the purpose of drawing His people back to Himself as they cried out to the LORD is Present in repentance.

Although the Israelites might have been tempted toward feelings of abandonment, the LORD never ceased to fill the heavens and the earth. He is constantly holding all things together and was never limited to a temple made by human hands. As the Israelites discerned a lack of the LORD's presence, we are often tempted to believe that the LORD is not near. We must rest in the truths that He is intimately acquainted with all of our ways (Ps. 139:3) and He has enclosed us behind and before and laid His hand upon us (Ps. 139:5). There is nowhere that we can go to flee from His Presence. Today, remember that your very breath comes from the LORD Is Present (Job 27:3). He is closer than your skin. He is with you always.

WEDNESDAY AND THURSDAY (DAY 3 AND 4): YHWH SHAMMAH

Over the next two days, we will study select passages surrounding the restoration of the manifest glory of God among His people. As we read about the presence of the LORD returning to the temple in Jerusalem, consider the description of the LORD's presence at Mount Sinai whenever Moses received the ten commandments: There was thunder, rumblings, lightnings, a thick cloud, a very loud trumpet blast, trembling in the Presence, and smoke (Exod. 19:16-20). A similar description of His Presence can be found in Exodus 24 before the LORD Is There says "and let them make me a sanctuary, that I may dwell in their midst" (Exod. 25:8) illustrating YHWH Shammah's desire to be manifest among His people.

Having departed from His people due to their unfathomable wickedness and His good justice, YHWH remained concerned about His own and is "very jealous for Jerusalem." He promised: "I will return to Jerusalem with mercy, and there My house will be rebuilt" (Zech. 1:14, 16). It becomes clear that everything that YHWH Shammah did was with the ultimate goal of restoring His people and His presence. God had not abandoned His people; rather, He went into exile with them for a time with the promise of creating a new heart and spirit within His beloved. No amount of wickedness cancels YHWH Shammah's nature. He is to be actualized among His people in a real, tangible way. As you study, praise the LORD Is There for being present in the Israelites' lives despite their wickedness. The implication of this truth is that He is present in your life despite your behavior. His Presence is an aspect of His identity and cannot be changed by our failures. And this is very good news for us all!

READ EZEKIEL 36:22-36.
What is the foundational reason given for God's actions on Israel's behalf?

What does the LORD promise to do externally/physically in regard to the Israelites?

What does the LORD promise to do internally in regard to the Israelites?

What do you think is meant by the phrases "new heart" and a "new spirit" in verse 26? (See also, Deut. 30:6, Ps. 51:10, John 3:3-5, and 2 Cor. 5:17.)

How does the LORD want the Israelites to respond to His mighty acts (vs. 31-32)?

Why do you think that the LORD seeks this response from His people? (See also, 1 John 1:9 and Acts 3:19.)

In verse 35, what does the LORD promise will become of Israel's land?

Has the LORD ever brought about undeserved restoration into your life? Explain.

READ EZEKIEL 43:1-5.
What description is given of the glory of the LORD?

In the vision, what does God's glory/manifest presence fill?

In Ezekiel 44:4, what was Ezekiel's response to the LORD's glory filling the temple?

What do you think your response should be to the LORD's presence?

READ EZEKIEL 48:35.
What new name is ascribed to Jerusalem?

How does the LORD describe His unchanging character in the new name given to His holy city?

There is hope for the Israelites. There is hope for Jerusalem. There is hope for all who belong to the LORD Is There. Because of His holiness and His great name, the LORD chooses to make His people clean by removing their hearts of stone and filling them with new hearts and spirits. This promise of putting His Spirit within His people (Ezek. 36:27) points to the inward work that the Father would do in sending the Holy Spirit in Jesus' name to indwell believers after Jesus' death, burial, resurrection, and ascension to the Father. For one to be able to walk in the LORD's statutes and obey His rules, one must be made completely new —one must become a new creation with new affections and desires. God alone can create a clean heart that loves YHWH and His commands. Only YHWH is capable of renewing a right spirit within mankind. In the context of Ezekiel's prophesies, we find that YHWH Shammah's Spirit has the power to bring people from sin to cleanliness in the sight of

God. YHWH's life-giving Spirit is able to bring dead people back to life and change people from the inside out.

In light of the work that YHWH Shammah does within His people, He is able to reside with His people. The restoration of YHWH Shammah's glory within the temple was an exhilarating vision for Ezekiel. He experienced the sound of many waters which speaks to the rushing nature of His returning presence and the earth shone brightly with the glory of the LORD. The LORD has set in His heart to "dwell in the midst of the people of Israel forever" (Ezek. 43:7). True believers have been grafted into God's family (Rom. 11:17) because if one belongs to Christ, then they are considered Abraham's descendants — a part of symbolic Israel (Gal. 3:29). Whoever the LORD has created a new heart and new spirit within is the one in which YHWH will dwell in their midst forever. Ezekiel's response to the vision of the glory of the LORD filling the temple was to fall on His face (Ezek. 44:4). We too must be in awe of the presence of YHWH among us and fall at His feet in worship. We must not become complacent and forget that He knows our every thought, hears our every word, and observes our every action. He is in the room as we engage in any sin, and He hears every careless word that comes out of our mouths. He is with us, and as we seek His help, He will help us live in light of His tangible presence.

FRIDAY (DAY 5): REFLECTION

Using the passages studied throughout the week, prayerfully answer the following reflection questions.

> Reflect upon and describe the difference that God's Presence has made in your outward circumstances.

Reflect upon and describe the difference that God's Presence has made in your heart, spirit, mind, and soul.

Do you feel like your secret sins escape the LORD's notice? How does the reality of YHWH's nature as present help you battle the temptation associated with secret sins?

If you truly lived every moment of your life believing that the LORD Is Present, what would change about your actions, thoughts, and speech?

MONDAY AND TUESDAY (DAY 6 AND 7): THE NEW JERUSALEM

In the last verse within the book of Ezekiel, Jerusalem is named "YHWH Shammah, the LORD is There" by God Himself. Name changes within the Bible often represent a special calling. Abram's name was changed to Abraham as the LORD confirmed His covenant with Abraham that Abraham would be a father to many nations. Abraham was called to be a father to the multitudes. Saul's name was changed to Paul after His radical conversion to the Christian faith and call to ministry with the Gentile nations. Paul was called to share the Gospel with pagan nations. Jerusalem's name was changed to the LORD Is There. This represents Jerusalem's calling to be filled with the Presence of God. Jerusalem certainly represents all who belong to the LORD past, present, and future. Consequently, all of God's people will experience the actualization of God's presence because that is the LORD's true character forever. The name changes and subsequent callings were not granted to Abraham, Paul, and Jerusalem because of their merit or incredible righteousness; every name change and calling depended upon the LORD and His purposes. All was for His glory and by His power.

YHWH Shammah is not the only new name ascribed to Jerusalem. Later it is called, "New Jerusalem" in Revelation 21. In the New Jerusalem, God Himself is present among all who believed in Jesus as their Lord and Savior. The LORD will be so near to His people that He will be able to physically touch and dwell among them in their heavenly home. Jerusalem's name change to YHWH Shammah foreshadowed the actualization of this calling to come at the end of age whenever the redeemed enter into the New Jerusalem … Heaven. Throughout the next two days, you will read passages that describe believers' future home with God Himself in the New Jerusalem. As you study, ask the Holy Spirit to remind you of the amazing truth that the LORD Is Present among His people and that He promises a day in which we will see Him face to face. Maybe you have loved ones that have already died in Christ and have entered into Heaven. As you study, think about their citizenship in Heaven and the closeness that they are experiencing to YHWH.

READ REVELATION 21:1-5.
What does John see in his vision in verses 1 and 2?

In your own words, what does God say in verses 3 and 4?

At what volume does He say it? Why do you think this might be significant in light of how God spoke to Elijah in 1 Kings 19:11-12?

What are the implications of God's presence among His people?

Which is the most encouraging to you and why?

How was this event foreshadowed in Leviticus 26:11-12 and Ezekiel 37:27-28?

READ REVELATION 21:22-27.
What was in the old Jerusalem that was not in the New Jerusalem?

Who is the temple?

Why does the New Jerusalem have no need for the sun or moon?

What other descriptions are given in regard to the New Jerusalem?

READ REVELATION 22:1-5.
Where did the river of the water of life flow from?

What might this river represent? (See also, John 4:10-14, 7:38-39, and Ezek. 36:25-27.)

How many thrones are mentioned in this passage? Who is sitting on the thrones?

The people of God "will see His face and His name will be on their foreheads. Read Exod. 33:20-23 and 34:29-35 and explain why this is a blessing.

Using verse 5, describe the impact of YHWH Shammah among His people. (See also, 1 Tim. 6:16.)

The New Jerusalem captures God's goal in sending Jesus as the atoning sacrifice for sins. The Holy One who cannot be in the presence of sin, made a way for the "dwelling place of God" to be "with man" (Rev. 21:3). The idea of God's presence tangibly among His people was foreshadowed in the tabernacle and temple, yet only the high priest was able to enter the Presence once a year. In the New Jerusalem, God is truly with His people and able to physically touch them as He wipes away every tear from their eyes (Rev. 21:4). Everything will occur just as YHWH Shammah had declared to Ezekiel thousands of years ago, "My dwelling place shall be with them, and I will be their God, and they shall be my people. Then the nations will know that I am the LORD who sanctifies Israel, when my sanctuary is in their midst forevermore" (Ezek. 37:27-28). In the New Jerusalem, there is no need for a physical temple because the LORD Is There is the temple and the light for all whose names are found written in the Lamb's book of life.

The river of the water of life described in Revelation 22:1-5 flows from the throne of God and through the middle of the street of the city. This description matches Ezekiel's vision of the future temple in Ezekiel 47. As the water flowed from the temple in Ezekiel's vision, the water flows from the throne of God in the New Jerusalem. Both illustrations point to the idea that the presence of God flows outwardly to bring life to all in the city. The water is a picture of how the LORD's Presence heals, refreshes, nourishes, and gives life to all. In the New Jerusalem, the people will be so acquainted with the LORD Is There that they will "see his face" (Rev. 22:4). This is an amazing truth knowing that even Moses could not see the Lord's face and live (Exod. 33 and 34). Moses used to speak to the LORD as a man speaks to his friend (Exod. 33:11), yet he was only permitted to see the back of the LORD's glory after the LORD had passed by, lest Moses die. Knowing that one day believers will be able to see the LORD in His glory, face to face, is one of the reasons that the saints are able to endure suffering on the earth with an unwavering hope in the promise of eternity in Heaven. What hope and joy awaits believers in the Kingdom to come as they will enjoy YHWH Shammah in His fullness. As we apply these truths to our lives, when we grieve the loss of a fellow believers, we will do so with hope (1 Thes. 4:13). Whether we die in Christ or are left until the coming of the LORD, one day we will all be caught up together in the clouds to meet the LORD and be with Him always and forever (1 Thes. 4:17).

WEDNESDAY AND THURSDAY (DAY 8 AND 9): THE HOLY SPIRIT

Throughout the past two weeks we have looked back on the tangible presence of God among the Israelites, and we have looked forward to the New Jerusalem and the incredible closeness believers will experience to the LORD Is Present in Heaven. Over the next two days, we will focus on the implications of YHWH Shammah in the lives of Christians through the power of the Holy Spirit. The Holy Spirit did not indwell believers until after Jesus ascended to the Father although specific individuals throughout history experienced the Holy Spirit "coming upon them" or "filling them" for specific purposes. In these occasions, the Holy Spirit did not remain within them. While Jesus was on the earth, He promised to send a Helper, the Holy Spirit, to His disciples (John 14:26). His Spirit was a gift to His people so that they could continue to walk in intimacy with YHWH.

The original outpouring of His Spirit happened at Pentecost in Jerusalem. 40 days after Jesus' ascension to Heaven, the disciples were gathered together in an upper room when "they were all filled with the Holy Spirit and began to speak with other tongues, as the Spirit gave them utterance" (Acts 2:4). There were many people gathered at Pentecost from different language backgrounds; therefore, by the power of the Spirit, all that were gathered were able to hear the Good News of Jesus Christ in their native tongue. The result of the initial outpouring of the Holy Spirit was 3000 saved souls (Acts 2:41). The Holy Spirit has many benefits in the lives of believers as they seek to follow Jesus and spread the Gospel of Jesus Christ. As you study, praise YHWH Shammah that we have been given rebirth and renewal by the Holy Spirit and that the Spirit was poured out on us generously through Jesus Christ our Savior (Titus 3:4-6). Ask yourself, how acquainted are you with the third part of the Triune God?

READ JOHN 14:15-31.
What will Jesus ask the Father to give to believers?

How often will the Helper's presence be with believers?

List the various names and descriptions given to the Holy Spirit with references.

How would you describe the difference between the Holy Spirit dwelling with a believer and being in a believer? (See also, 1 Cor. 3:16 and Eph. 1:13.)

Describe an orphan. What do you think Jesus means when he says, "I will not leave you as orphans" (vs. 16)? (See also, Rom. 8:14-16.)

Who does Jesus say He will manifest Himself to?

Note: The Geek word for "home" is also used in John 14:2 whenever Jesus describes His Father's House and the rooms that are being prepared for believers in Heaven.

Describe "home." What do you think Jesus means when He says, "we will come to him and make our home with him" (vs. 23)?

Where do you find evidence of the trinity in this passage of Scripture?

What two roles did Jesus say that the Helper would fulfill in the lives of believers?

What truths can you cling to when you feel tempted to disobey Jesus' command to "let not your hearts be troubled, nether let them be afraid" (vs. 27)?

READ JOHN 16:4-15.
What reason does Jesus give His disciples to explain how it is to their advantage that He go away?

What does Jesus say the Holy Spirit will do whenever He comes?

What clarifications does Jesus add about the Holy Spirit convicting the world of sin, righteousness, and judgment? What do you think Jesus means by each clarification?

What did Jesus withhold from His disciples, and what reason does He give for doing so?

What will the Spirit of Truth do?

READ 1 CORINTHIANS 12:11.
What does the Spirit give to believers?

Who is responsible for empowering believers to have gifts, walk in service, and carry out various activities within ministry?

Why is each believer given a manifestation of the Spirit?

What are the gifts of the Spirit outlined in this passage?

According to verse 11, what is the Spirit's job?

READ 1 CORINTHIANS 2:9-16, ACTS 1:8, AND EPHESIANS 1:17-20.
What additional truths do you glean
in regard to YHWH Shammah?

Instead of being housed in a temple made my human hands, YHWH Shammah chose to make His people His temple so that He could dwell within them (1 Cor. 3:16). The beauty of this truth reveals the character and desire of God to reveal Himself to His people and continually provide them with His life-giving presence. All praise to the LORD Is There for not only indwelling believers but always being with them as He sets His seal upon them claiming them as His own possession (2 Cor. 1:22). The world is acquainted with grief in regard to loneliness, lack of belonging, and abandonment. YHWH Shammah does not leave His people as orphans; He makes His home with them. Forever, the Father and the Son ensured that their family would be cared for, provided for, and close to Him through the Holy Spirit.

The benefits of the Holy Spirit are so vast that Jesus explained to His disciples that it was to their advantage that He returns to His father so that the Holy Spirit would be sent to them. It is hard to imagine how something could be more advantageous than the physical presence of

Jesus among people, but the infinite God has an infinite Spirit capable of simultaneously reaching every heart belonging to God. Additionally, we praise God because the Holy Spirit is responsible for helping believers understand His Word (Col. 1:9), reminding individuals of Jesus' words (John 14:26), and revealing to them the thoughts of God (1 Cor. 2:11). Only the Holy Spirit is able to reveal man's sinfulness so that one will repent and be saved. The Holy Spirit reveals that there is a righteous standard only met by Jesus that we could never meet, and the Holy Spirit reveals that there is a judgment to come; therefore, we must repent and be saved (John 16:8). Additionally, the Holy Spirit appoints to Christians a variety of gifts through the manifestation of His Spirit for the common good of all people. He empowers believers with whatever He determines is needed in order for a believer to carry out the services and activities for which the LORD has called them. These are astounding, undeserved benefits of being indwelled by the Holy Spirit. Praise YHWH Shammah because He is omnipresent, inhabits His people, and will one day be fully actualized before their very eyes in the New Jerusalem. He alone is worthy of praise for counting sinners worthy of His Presence.

FRIDAY (DAY 10): REFLECTION

Honestly and thoughtfully answer the following reflections questions.

What details about the New Jerusalem encourage you the most as you anticipate your future home in Heaven?

In what ways have you experienced the work of the Holy Spirit in your life? Write a prayer of Thanksgiving for His closeness to you at all times.

What gifts has the Holy Spirit given you? How can you use the gifts that the LORD Is There has bestowed upon you for His Kingdom?

LESSON 9: YHWH RAAH, THE LORD IS MY SHEPHERD

It is utterly shocking for the LORD to be ascribed the name, "My Shepherd," due to the cultural view of shepherds in the time of which the Bible was written. Historically, shepherds were viewed as lowly, poor, dirty, and unintelligent. They were nobodies performing a job that anyone could accomplish from their youth. There was little respect for the office of a shepherd. Surprisingly, the LORD used shepherds to accomplish large, seemingly impossible tasks throughout history. King David was only a shepherd boy when He was anointed the next King of Israel by the prophet Samuel and was still a shepherd when he defeated Goliath in the name of the LORD of Hosts. Moses was a shepherd of his father-in-law's flocks whenever the great I AM spoke to him in a burning bush and told him to return to Egypt and lead the Israelites out of bondage and to the Promised Land. After Jesus was born, God chose to reveal the incarnation of God Himself as a newborn baby by sending a host of angels to shepherds in a nearby field.

Truly, God chooses what is foolish in the eyes of the world to shame the wise. God choose those that are weak to shame the strong (1 Cor. 1:27). Truly, "whoever exalts himself will be humbled, and whoever humbles himself will be exalted" (Matt. 23:12). Throughout Scripture we find countless examples of God using the weak to shame the strong, humbling the proud, and exalting the humble. The LORD Is My Shepherd consistently chooses those of lowly status in the eyes of the world to do great things through the power of God for the glory of God on the earth.

YHWH Raah doesn't simply use shepherds to accomplish His purposes, He attaches their title to His personal name. He is infinitely and perfectly the Shepherd of His flock. Shepherds were charged with the responsibilities of caring for the flock by leading them toward their basic needs such as areas with vegetation and water. Shepherds defended the flock from predators, and shepherds ensured the safety and well-being of the entire flock by going after any sheep that strayed away from the flock. Knowing the role of a shepherd helps in understanding why "Raah" was attached to the LORD's personal name. YHWH both leads and cares for His flock, Israel and ultimately all who will believe including both Jews and Gentiles, as He leads His sheep toward their needs. He provides and cares for His flock perfectly and consistently. As the flock faces trials, threats, and danger, the LORD Is My Shepherd defends and protects both the strong and weak sheep of His pasture. If a member of the flock goes astray, the Shepherd is faithful to ensure they are returned safely to their flock.

Although the LORD Is My Shepherd is not poor, unintelligent, and to be overlooked by society as unimportant, like human shepherds, He is gentle and lowly in heart (Matt. 11:29). Jesus Christ, though He was God, made himself nothing and took on the form of a servant. He humbled Himself to the point of utter humiliation as He died on the cross (Phil. 2:7-8). It is because of His sacrifice, despite His position and status, that He is to be highly exalted, bowed before, and given the name above every name (Phil. 2:9-10). Throughout this study, ask the LORD Is My Shepherd to show you His character and cultivate love in your heart for the One that provides for, leads, and protects you. Ask Him to remind your heart that He doesn't overlook the poor and lowly but uses those of humble heart.

MONDAY AND TUESDAY (DAY 1 AND 2): THE LORD IS MY SHEPHERD

Throughout the next two days, you will be studying Psalm 23. In the passage, YHWH is referred to as "My Shepherd" by the psalmist, King David. The first four verses of this chapter describe the LORD and His divine character as the Shepherd while the last two verses focus on the LORD in relation to mankind as He invites faithful followers to join Him as guests at His table for all eternity as they dwell together in the house of YHWH. In this passage, YHWH Raah is praised as the one who provides for and satisfies the sheep of His flock. He provides His sheep with soul refreshment and leadership toward paths of life and peace, yet Scripture makes it clear that sometimes the sheep find themselves face to face with "the valley of the shadow of death" (Ps. 23:4). In the midst of difficult circumstances, the sheep find themselves comforted by the discipline and leadership of the Good Shepherd.

Eventually, in His perfect timing, the shadow of death will come for all mankind. Death is inevitable, but death is powerless against the members of YHWH Raah's flock because death on earth leads to the sheep "dwelling in the house of the LORD forever." When a sheep dies in Christ, they replace their pasture full of valleys and dark paths with a prepared table, overflowing cup, and fellowship with the Merciful One for days without end. "Oh death, where is your sting" (1 Cor. 15:55)? As you study Psalm 23, ask YHWH Raah to reveal His divine character as your shepherd as He reminds you that He desires fellowship with you at His table as members of His family. Remember as you face valleys to give praise to YHWH because He is the Father of compassion and the God of all comfort. He is faithful to comfort, lead, and protect you in your troubles so that you can comfort others with the comfort that you receive from God as His sheep (2 Cor. 1:3).

READ PSALM 23.
What is the role of a shepherd and how does it relate to the LORD's identity as "My Shepherd?" (See also, 1 Sam. 17:34-36.)

How does the LORD Is My Shepherd keep us from wanting? (See also, Ps. 34:9-10 and Matt. 6:33.)

The Shepherd makes His sheep lie down in "green pastures" and leads them "beside still waters." What do you think is meant by these two metaphors?

Special Note: The soul typically refers to the mind, will, and emotions of a person.

What connection can be made between the restoration of one's soul and being led on paths of righteousness? (See also, Ps. 19:7.)

What reason is given for the sheep being led on paths of righteousness?

Choose at least one of the following passages: 1 Samuel 17:1-54, 1 Samuel 19:1-20:42, or 2 Samuel 15:1-17. Describe an event in which David faced literal danger that could have resulted in His death?

Choose at least one of the following passages: 2 Samuel 12:15-23, 2 Samuel 13:23-33, or 2 Samuel 18:1-33. What event was David led through by God in which He faced deep darkness and death in an emotional sense?

What truths comforted David as He walked through the "valley of the shadow of death?"

Read the following references: Proverbs 13:24, Hebrews 12:5-6. What do you think is meant by the Shepherd's rod?

Read the following passages and list the uses of the shepherd's staff: Exodus 4:17, 7:20, 14:21 and Numbers 20:7-10. What deeper spiritual connections do you make between a shepherd's staff and the comfort His staff provides to His sheep?

What valleys and shadows of death have you personally experienced? How can you apply the truths listed above to your circumstances?

Using verse 5, what does the LORD Is My Shepherd do for His sheep?

What do you think it means that the Shepherd "prepares a table before [us]?"

What other tables does the LORD invite His sheep to partake in according to Matthew 26:26-29 and Revelation 19:6-9?

Who are the Christian's enemies according to Ephesians 6:12?

What is the significance of the LORD
is My Shepherd preparing a table in the
presence of Christians' enemies?

Note: Throughout the Bible, people were anointed with oil for a special purpose or call. (Exodus 29:7, Exodus 40:9, 2 Kings 9:6, Ecclesiastes 9:8, James 5:14)

READ 1 JOHN 2:18-21.
With what are Christians anointed and for what purpose are Christians given the anointing?

READ 1 JOHN 2:26-27.
What impact does Jesus' anointing have in the life of a believer?

READ PSALM 23:6-7.
List specific examples of ways in which the Good Shepherd has caused your cup to overflow or give examples of ways in which God has shown you goodness and mercy.

Consider the days without end that the sheep will experience with the LORD Is My Shepherd. How does this truth help you combat anxiousness and depression?

Throughout Psalm 23, YHWH is seen as the caretaker, guidance-giver, provider, protector, and leader of the flock. Such a realization results in the believer's peace as they recognize that the pressure to provide, protect, and lead does not fall on their shoulders — those jobs fall on the capable shoulders of the Good Shepherd. The LORD of peace Himself gives peace at all times and in every way (2 Thes. 3:16), and Christians do well to focus upon this reality. YHWH Raah is faithful to restore our anxious minds and unsettled emotions as He leads us down paths of righteousness. Truly, obedience to the commands of God revives the soul and produces peace. YHWH Raah's commands are not burdens but life-giving leading for all who follow on paths of righteousness. As a sheep is led down paths of righteousness, the reputation of the true God is preserved, and His character is revealed through the righteousness of His flock members.

David, the author of Psalm 23, was one acquainted with life-threatening situations and deep, emotional pain. He could have been referring to any number of events when he stated that he "walks through the valley of the shadow of death" (Ps. 23:4). He could have died at the hands of Goliath and the Philistine army, perished as Saul relentlessly pursued His life, or perished as his own son, Absalom, sought to kill him to take his place as king. David did not only face physical threats but was well-acquainted with emotional grief. David's sins of adultery and murder resulted in the death of his newborn child, he faced the betrayal and hatred from his older sons as they pursued their own success, and he faced grief as his children made horrific, sinful decisions that resulted in their deaths. Through all of these circumstances, David found himself comforted by the rod and staff of YHWH Raah. YHWH Raah's discipline (rod) and leadership (staff) caused David to be free from the fear of evil in the midst of the valley of the shadow of death.

In the same way that David was comforted, those belonging to YHWH Raah can be comforted by the same truths. YHWH Raah prepares a table for His own in the presence of their enemies, anoints their heads with oil, and causes their cups to overflow. This table most certainly speaks to the Marriage Supper of the Lamb that is to come as believers are gathered to Heaven with the Shepherd of their souls, but it also speaks to an intimate relationship with the Shepherd on earth. It is a rare occurrence for one to share a meal and a table with total strangers; rather, we are acquainted with dining with our close family and friends. YHWH Raah's preparing of a table is an invitation to an intimate relationship with Himself where conversation is shared by family. The Shepherd wants to know and be known by His sheep. A personal relationship with the Shepherd is one characterized by constant overflow of mercy and goodness in spite of the flock's wanderings. Are you taking time to grow in your relationship with your Shepherd? Ask the LORD to prune and refine your heart so that you are obedient to Him and experience the "overflowing" nature of knowing YHWH Raah.

WEDNESDAY AND THURSDAY (DAY 3 AND 4): YHWH RAAH'S RESPONSE TO A NEGLECTED FLOCK

Ezekiel 34 speaks to YHWH's nature as YHWH Raah, the LORD Is My Shepherd. In the first 16 verses of this chapter, the prophet of Israel describes the current shepherds of Israel, outlines their actions, and speaks to their condemnation. Then, the LORD describes in detail the ways in which He would seek out and search for His flock that had been scattered. The use of "shepherds" in this passage is a metaphor for the rulers of Israel. The LORD appointed shepherds for Israel and appoints shepherds (pastors) of churches today to provide for the needs of the sheep. Shepherds are overseers of a flock. Shepherds are charged with the care, protection, and leadership of the flock; therefore, it is noteworthy that the Preeminent Shepherd, God Himself, brings charges against the leadership for their utter failure in caring for and leading the flock. Israel's shepherds neglected the sheep and raised themselves above the sheep at the cost of the sheep. While these failed shepherds elevated themselves, they tread upon the sheep pushing them into lack. They turned their backs on the hungry, weak, sick, injured, strayed, and lost. Their actions were in direct opposition to the character of the LORD Is My Shepherd. As YHWH Raah pronounces a rescuing of the sheep, the justice and care of YHWH is displayed.

As you study YHWH Raah's response to the misery of his neglected flock, ask the Holy Spirit to reveal the ways in which the LORD Is My Shepherd has gathered, rescued, fed, established, and taken care of you throughout your life. As you study remember the words of Jesus, "Fear not, little flock, for it is the Father's good pleasure to give you the kingdom" (Luke 12:32). The LORD Is My Shepherd never leaves His post. He is committed to you, a sheep of His flock. His care for each individual sheep in His flock is so great that "we can confidently say, 'the LORD is my helper; I will not fear'" (Heb. 13:6).

READ EZEKIEL 34:1-6.
What are the charges the LORD has against Israel's shepherds/leaders?

What does the LORD state should
have been done for His sheep?

What is the result of the shepherds'/
leaders' lack of care for the flock?

READ EZEKIEL 34:7-10.
In what ways were the shepherds punished
by the LORD Is My Shepherd?

What evidence of the Good Shepherd's
justice do you find in this passage?

READ EZEKIEL 34:11-16.
In verse 11, what two things does the
LORD say that He will do?

Re-read Psalm 23. What similarities do you find between Psalm 23 and Ezekiel 34:11-16?

What aspects of Ezekiel 34:11-16 point to the LORD Is My Shepherd's provision?

What aspects of Ezekiel 34:11-16 point to the LORD Is My Shepherd's protection?

What aspects of Ezekiel 34:11-16 point to the LORD Is My Shepherd's peace?

What aspects of Ezekiel 34:11-16 point to the LORD Is My Shepherd's goodness?

What aspects of Ezekiel 34:11-16 point to
the LORD Is My Shepherd's mercy?

Make a list of things that YHWH Raah
promises to do for His sheep.

Which promise means the most to you and why?

While throughout history, human shepherds have failed to fulfill their responsibilities to the flock by strengthening the weak, healing the sick, nursing the wounds of the injured, bringing back the strayed, and seeking after the lost, YHWH Raah will never neglect His flock and act contrary to His infinite, unchanging character. The LORD Is My Shepherd's nature is to search out those that belong to Himself that have been scattered. He takes seriously the care of His flock and chooses to rescue them from every place in which they have been driven or have strayed. The LORD speaks of rescuing His sheep from all the "places where they have been scattered on the day of clouds and thick darkness" (Ezek. 34:12). As we relate this passage to our lives, we too experience days of clouds and thick darkness. Circumstances, trials, temptations, and sinful behavior are often used by Satan to isolate sheep from their flock and cause them to stray from the care of the LORD Is My Shepherd. Thankfully, the Shepherd is the master seeker and saver of the flock. He Himself chooses and will always choose to search for, seek out, and rescue His own.

Once the sheep have been brought back to the flock, YHWH Raah delivers the sheep from their anxieties and fears as He causes them to lie down in peace because He is their capable protector. The sheep of the LORD's flock are fully cared for; therefore, they do not have to worry and stress about their lives. Instead of anxiously striving, the sheep should lay down their burdens at their Shepherd's feet. As followers of YHWH Raah come to faith in His character as the Shepherd, they find peace in the knowledge of His sufficient protection and provision. In His goodness, the LORD Is My Shepherd binds up the injured, strengthens the weak, and destroys the enemy while providing justice to those that have been mistreated and abused. The Shepherd never abandons His flock but blesses them continually with His presence. All that belong to Him know the intimacy that is shared between Shepherd and sheep. His mercy is revealed in that sheep are prone to stray and cause their own injuries and weakness, yet, instead of neglecting them and justly forsaking them due to their sin, the LORD Is My Shepherd has mercy upon the sheep of His flock and brings them back into His fold. Today, recognize that you were deserving of being forsaken by the Shepherd. Instead of leaving you, He sought you out, rescued you from His just wrath against your sin, and has cared for you perfectly all the days of your life.

FRIDAY (DAY 5): REFLECTION

Today, reflect upon the ways in which you are prone to wander away from the boundaries that YHWH Raah has provided you in His Word. Write down the common temptations that you experience that draw you away from the goodness, provision, protection, and peace of the LORD Is My Shepherd.

For each identified temptation, write down one verse from the Bible that you can cling to in the midst of temptation.

MONDAY AND TUESDAY (DAY 6 AND 7): YHWH RAAH'S PROMISES TO HIS FLOCK

In Ezekiel 34:1-16, YHWH Raah was addressing the negligent leaders of God's people. He pronounced condemnation due to their lack of fulfillment in regard to their role as a shepherd and then explained how He would restore the scattered flock to Himself. In Ezekiel 34:17-24, YHWH Raah addresses those belonging to the flock rather than the leaders of the flock. He strongly reproves ill-treatment within the flock brought about by members of the flock. Those part of a church body certainly relate to wounds inflicted by fellow members of the congregation. It is through this passage that we are both warned and encouraged as sheep. Warned because YHWH Raah does not take lightly behaviors within the flock such as selfish greed at the expense of the other sheep. Instead of being grateful for their position within the flock as provided-for, some flock members were prone to "push with side and shoulder" and "thrust at all the weak with horns" (Ezek. 34:21). This type of pushing and shoving will be judged by the Good Shepherd — injustice does not escape His notice. The flock can be encouraged that their true leader, YHWH Raah's, character is to reward those that feed the hungry, give drink to the thirsty, welcome the stranger, clothe the naked, and visit the sick and imprisoned (Matt. 25:31-46).

In the second portion of the passage, Ezekiel announces the coming of a Davidic Shepherd. This prophesy would sound familiar to the Israelites because Ezekiel's predecessor, Jeremiah, had spoken words from the LORD in regard to the coming Davidic Messiah, the righteous Branch of David, In Jeremiah 23:5. "… I will raise up for David a righteous

Branch, and He shall reign as king and deal wisely, and shall execute justice and righteousness in the land." Both prophesies point to the Christ. One that is both fully Divine and human in nature — coming from the line of King David. These prophesies are foundational to the Jewish faith as Jews centered their lives around waiting and praying for the Messiah because it was prophesied that He would establish "a covenant of peace" and "banish wild beasts from the land," and cause the people to "dwell securely" (Ezek. 34:25).

The final portion of the passage gives further details into the blessings that would come from the Messianic, Davidic, Christ to come and Shepherd the flock. As you study, it is important to remember that the Jewish audience for which this passage was written to (yet the passage remains for us), interpreted the coming Shepherd to be one that would come and conquer their enemies by force and then sit down on a throne to rule over them. They did not understand that the covenant of peace would be one between God and man through the blood of Christ. They did not know that the oppression and slavery to end would be the bondage of sin and death that afflicted the people. As you study, ask the Shepherd of your soul to remind you that you are His sheep, and He is your Shepherd — you are claimed by God and for God.

READ EZEKIEL 34:17-22.
What victimization seems to be occurring within the flock?

Can you think of any modern-day examples of this type of behavior within the church?

Why do you think the LORD takes seriously the wrongs done by sheep to other sheep? (See also, Rom. 12:4-5, 14:19, John 13:35.)

READ EZEKIEL 34:23-24.
In your own words, what did Ezekiel prophesy?

What connection does Jesus have to David and the prophesied position this "David" would hold? (See also, Matt. 1:1 and Luke 1:32-33.)

Read the following passages where Jesus is referred to as "the son of David:" Matthew 12:22-23, Matthew 21:9, Mark 10:46 - 52, Romans 1:3-5, and Revelation 5:5.
What correlations do you find between the prophesy about the long-awaited Messiah, the promised "one shepherd, my servant David" (vs. 23) that would be "prince among them" (vs. 24) and Jesus?

Note: Remember that these verses follow a Messianic prophesy; therefore, the promises and covenant made will be fulfilled with the coming of the Shepherd — the Messiah.

READ EZEKIEL 34:25-31.
What specific type of covenant does the LORD make with His sheep?

What was the goal of "banishing wild beasts from the land?"

What might be examples of the figurative language "wild beasts" that hinder Christians from dwelling securely and being at peace?

Who and what does the LORD make a blessing?

What does the LORD send upon His sheep?

What acts performed by YHWH Raah cause
the sheep to know that He is the LORD?

Describe a time in which the LORD Is My
Shepherd delivered you from enslavement to a
particular sin. How did this increase your faith?

Using verses 28-29, how would you describe
the LORD's heart toward His sheep?

Using verses 30-31, what seems to be a
priority for the Good Shepherd?

The LORD Is My Shepherd spoke to Ezekiel in regard to His plan to care for the needs of His flock. This plan included ways in which flock members were to treat one another. The LORD Is My Shepherd exhorted the sheep not to push, mistreat, and insist upon their own way; rather, they were to pursue mutual upbuilding since they were all members of the same flock. Today, many people recount leaving churches due to hurtful behavior from fellow church members. The Good Shepherd judges rightly between sheep and sheep — He sees the full picture. It is important that the people of God's flock love one another deeply. In loving one another, a person proves that they are truly after the Shepherd's heart. If you find yourself in the middle of the flock (your church), and the Holy Spirit reveals to you that a fellow sheep has something against you, the LORD commands you to go and be reconciled to your brother or sister before offering your gift of worship to Himself (Matt. 5:32).

After the LORD's encouragement and exhortation for the sheep, He reveals His divine plan. He determined to set up one shepherd, a David, over the entire flock. By calling this Shepherd, "my servant, David" God revealed His plan to send a Shepherd that was fully human, yet the LORD follows up His Davidic statement with "I, the LORD, will be their God" pointing to the coming Shepherd's divine nature. Jesus explains the mystery of this prophesy as He declares Himself the Good Shepherd in John 10 which will be studied over the course of the next two days. Immediately after the Messianic prophesy, the LORD speaks verses 25-31 to the flock of Israel. These verses should be interpreted in light of the coming Good Shepherd, the Messiah. YHWH Raah states that He would make a covenant of peace with the flock. This prophesy was fulfilled by Jesus who made "peace by the blood of His cross." All were completely alienated from God, but Jesus reconciled the sheep to God by His atoning sacrifice on the cross (Col. 1:20-22). The LORD speaks of the Messianic age in which the Good Shepherd would shower His flock with blessings causing the fruits of the Holy Spirit to increase in the lives of the sheep. The coming Shepherd that manifested perfectly the character of YHWH Raah would be responsible for breaking oppressive yokes and delivering the flock from enslavement. Although the Jews interpreted this aspect of prophesy to mean a literal warfare-type takeover, Jesus did not come to establish an earthly kingdom. Jesus broke the oppressive power of sin. Romans 6:20 describes mankind as "slaves to sin," and Romans 8:2 states that Jesus came to "set us free ... from the law of sin and death." This type of reign and rule in the lives of believers is YHWH Raah's ultimate way of feeding, providing for, and protecting the sheep of His flock. The LORD Is My Shepherd's desire is that they would know that He is with them and that all who believe and follow Him are His people — human sheep of His pasture.

WEDNESDAY AND THURSDAY (DAY 8 AND 9): THE GOOD SHEPHERD

In the final portion of the YHWH Raah study, we will be studying John 10:1 -21. In this passage, Jesus makes one of His seven "I Am" statements recorded in the Gospel of John. He refers to Himself as the Good Shepherd. As the Jewish audience listened to Jesus' words, they would have understood this statement as a claim to deity due to Old Testament passages such as Psalm 23, Ezekiel 34, and Jeremiah 23 which depict God as the Shepherd of Israel: YHWH Raah. In addition to making Himself equal with God, in referring to Himself as the Good Shepherd, Jesus was making a claim to be the long-awaited Davidic Messiah prophesied in Jeremiah 23:1-4 and Ezekiel 34 — the one who would be the true Shepherd to the flock of Israel. The response to such claims from hearers would either be belief in Jesus as both God and Messiah or offense at what was perceived as blasphemy.

Although Jesus' claims would not be lost upon His Jewish audience, this passage is rich with metaphors. The sheepfold is an area in which neighboring families kept their sheep. The sheepfold represents the places in which God's people are located. The gate/door is either a door or an opening in which the sheep entered and exited the sheepfold. In this passage, Jesus is the "door/gate" by which the true sheep have access to God and His flock. Jesus makes a way through which people can have access to the provision and protection of YHWH Raah. The thief and robbers within this passage represent leaders of Israel that were tasked with tending to the needs of God's people, yet they fed and took care of themselves at the expense of God's people. The gatekeeper is the one that calls the sheep in and out of the sheep fold. Jesus is also the gatekeeper, and those that are His will recognize His voice and leading.

As you study this passage, ask YHWH Raah to help you understand the Good Shepherd's heart toward His flock and His authority. Ask the LORD Is My Shepherd to help you understand that through Jesus' willing sacrificial death, He proved Himself to be the door (our access to God in Heaven), gatekeeper (one in charge of who does and does not have access to Heaven), and the Good Shepherd.

READ JOHN 10:1-6
In what ways does Jesus describe the Good Shepherd?

In what ways does Jesus describe the thieves/robbers of the flock?

Thieves and robbers often act in secret with varying degrees of violence. How do Matthew 7:15, Matthew 24:24, and 2 Peter 2:1 help you understand what a "thief" might look like in the Church?

According to Jesus, what will "the sheep" do and know?

What are the actions of the Good Shepherd in relation to His flock?

How will the true sheep respond to anyone other than the Good Shepherd that seeks to lead them?

Jesus states that the sheep "know His voice" in John 10:4. How do the following verses, John 8:47 and James 1:22, further explain the way true sheep will respond to God's words?

According to the following verses, Isaiah 53:6 and 1 Peter 5:8, why are the sheep in need of the Good Shepherd?

READ JOHN 10:7-13

What does YHWH state is His name in Exodus 3:13-15?

Read John 6:35, John 8:12, John 10:7, John 11:25, John 10:11, John 14:6, and John 15:1. How do Jesus' "I am" statements relate to Exodus 3:13-15?

What are the purposes of a door? What do you think it means that Jesus is the door?

What is the result of entering through Jesus, the door?

What does the Good Shepherd give His sheep?

What does the Good Shepherd do for
His sheep? (See also, John 15:13.)

How do the thief and the hired hand treat
the sheep? How do these behaviors compare
with the behaviors of the Good Shepherd?

Describe the way Jesus, the Good Shepherd,
knows His sheep based upon the comparison
He made in verse 14. (See also, John 10:30.)

Read Matthew 28:18-20 and Ephesians 2:11-22, and
explain what Jesus meant when He stated that He has
"other sheep that are not of this fold" (John 10:16).

In light of verses 17-18, what does it mean to you that Jesus willingly died for you?

As we studied Ezekiel 34, the "flock" referred to Israel. In John 10, Jesus declared Himself as the Good Shepherd and stated that "if anyone enters by [Him], [they] would be saved ... and find pasture" (John 10:9). Anyone, Jew or Gentile, who enters by way of faith in Jesus Christ as Savior and Lord will be counted as one of YHWH Raah's sheep. In John 10:16, Jesus explains that He had other sheep that He had not brought into the fold yet. His plan was to make "disciples of all nations" (Matt. 28:19). There is no other way to be considered God's family outside of Jesus — He alone is the Door to salvation. He alone is the means through which we can find pasture with God. True sheep will never be deceived by other false "ways to God" or voices of thieves and robbers that seek to draw sheep away from their True Shepherd. True sheep can rest assured that Jesus goes before them, and that He has given them ears to hear His voice. The Good Shepherd is able to keep His sheep.

While the enemy, Satan, is always at work seeking to steal, kill, and destroy the flock, the Good Shepherd willingly lays down His life for His sheep so that the flock can experience eternal life. Jesus had all authority, but He chose to lay down His life on His own accord and become the "Lamb of God that takes away the sins of the world" (John 1:29). Jesus' life was not taken from Him; rather, He gave up His life willingly on behalf of the flock. We can be encouraged. If YHWH Raah is willing to die an excruciating death in our stead, what care, provision, protection, leadership, goodness, and mercy will He withhold from us? YHWH Raah was so bent upon seeking and rescuing His sheep that He chose the cross. It is due to His sacrifice that we are able to become one flock with one Shepherd with access to eternal life in Heaven with YHWH. Our only response can be that of worship and surrender to Jesus as our Master and Savior as He tends to us, cares for us, and leads us perfectly. "He will tend his flock like a shepherd; he will gather the lambs in his arms; he will carry them in his bosom, and gently lead those that are with young" (Is. 40:11).

FRIDAY (DAY 10): REFLECTION

Thinking back to the Scriptures studied throughout the week, prayerfully respond to the following reflection questions.

Review Matthew 5:21-24. Is there a fellow brother or sister in Christ that you need to be reconciled with? If so, write down a plan to pursue love and unity in the name of the Good Shepherd.

Make a list of YHWH Raah's never-changing, infinite character traits. Write down the Scripture references that support each characteristic you beheld throughout the past two weeks of Bible study.

Write a prayer of thanksgiving, adoration, and worship to YHWH Raah.

LESSON 10: YHWH ELOHIM AND YHWH HOSEENU, ETERNAL CREATOR AND THE LORD OUR MAKER

"In the beginning, God created the heavens and the earth. The earth was without form and empty, and darkness was over the face of the deep. And the Spirit of God was hovering over the face of the waters" (Gen. 1:1-2). Then, out of nothing, God brings everything that is into existence by His word. The Eternal Creator, YHWH Elohim, sets the entire creation in order and makes the earth a place for His presence. YHWH Elohim stands alone in power and authority because He alone possesses the ability to create anything out of nothing. The transcendence and power of God as Creator is beyond our ability to understand — "by faith we understand that the universe was created by the word of God, so that what is seen was not made out of things that are visible" (Heb. 11:3).

The word for God in Genesis 1:1, Elohim, is plural. This points to the triune nature of God — He is One who manifests Himself in three persons: God the Father, God the Son, and God the Holy Spirit. In the beginning, the entire Trinity created. In Genesis 1:27, God said, "Let us make man in our image, after our likeness ..." which makes the subject plural pointing again to the triune nature of God. This truth is echoed by the Apostle John in his Gospel account of Jesus Christ: "In the beginning was the Word, and the Word was with God, and the Word was God. He was in the beginning with God. All things were made through him, and without him was not anything made that was made" (John 1:1-3). The great Eternal Creator who has incomprehensible power, perfect wisdom, and is Triune in nature is the Creator of absolutely everything that exists.

While the name of God, YHWH Elohim speaks to His divine ability to create all things, the LORD is ascribed another name by the psalmist, King David (Heb. 4:7), in Psalm 95:6. David implores the congregation to "worship and bow down" and "kneel before the LORD Our Maker!" In Hebrew, the LORD Our Maker is YHWH Hoseenu. Both YHWH Elohim and YHWH Hoseenu describe the LORD's unchanging identity and character as the Maker, but the attachment of "Our Maker" to the LORD's personal name reminds us that we, mankind, were created. We have no life and power in and of ourselves. We were made in the image of YHWH. We were created after His likeness — both male and female (Gen. 1:26-27). As image-bearers of their Maker, humans have been given the capacity to understand morality, develop committed and loving relationships, express authority over creation, exhibit reason, and exercise creativity. Humans, made in the image of the Eternal Creator and the LORD Our Maker, have been given the opportunity to develop a relationship with God. When a third of the angels rebelled against God and followed Satan resulting in a heavenly war that ultimately led to Satan and his demonic armies being thrown out of Heaven, God did not take on their form, die in their stead, and make a way for them to be made right with Himself. When mankind rebelled against God in their sin, Jesus did take on the form of a man, suffered, died, and was raised to life to redeem and save His image bearers and restore relationship between God and man. This should move our hearts toward obedience to our loving Creator.

As Jesus, the second part of the Trinity, walked the earth as a man, He displayed the creating power of God by creating body parts as He healed the sick and diseased, multiplying loaves of bread and fish, and creating life within individuals pronounced dead. After the Holy Spirit, the third part of the Trinity, was sent, His work was and is to make new creations in Christ (2 Cor. 5:17) as believers are transformed into the image of Christ by the Spirit of God (2 Cor. 3:18). Throughout this study, ask the Holy Spirit to open your eyes and heart to understand His Triune nature. Ask YHWH Elohim to sanctify you in the truth as you study His unchanging and infinite character as the Eternal Creator. Ask YHWH Hoseenu to remind you that He is your Maker and that you bear His image in the world for His glory. "Worthy are you, our Lord and God, to receive glory and honor and power, for you created all things, and by your will they existed and were created" (Rev. 4:11).

MONDAY AND TUESDAY (DAY 1 AND DAY 2): THE CREATIONS

On the sixth day of creation, YHWH Elohim made mankind in His image and said, "Let them have dominion over the fish of the sea and over the birds of the heavens and over the livestock and over all the earth and over every creeping thing that creeps on the earth" (Gen. 1:26). YHWH, who is altogether sufficient and needless, created mankind in

His image and granted mankind the responsibility of exercising authority over the earth. The LORD did not create the heavens and earth to meet His own needs or fulfill a lack in His existence; rather, the LORD ultimately created mankind for His glory (Isa. 43:7). The people in which YHWH Elohim formed for Himself were created with the purpose of declaring His praise (Isa. 43:21). Before the Creation, YHWH Elohim chose humans to be holy and blameless before His Everlasting Presence and to be counted as sons and daughters. As God created mankind, He knew that mankind would fall into sin resulting in death. Yet, His plan of redemption for rebellious mankind was His will from the beginning. Creation, the Fall of mankind, Redemption through the blood of Jesus, the judgment of the earth, and the creation of the New Heaven and New Earth were and are for the glory and praise of Himself (Eph. 1:3-6).

In Genesis 1:28, YHWH Elohim blessed males and females saying, "be fruitful and multiply." If the Eternal Creator who merely speaks and the galaxies spin into motion, vegetation rises from the earth, and all kinds of wildlife appears blesses mankind with His words, we can be certain that they will be exactly as He has declared. They will be fruitful, and they will multiply. In this blessing, we find God's design for mankind — that image bearers who reflect His characteristics would represent God on the Earth in governing over creation and building meaningful relationships with Himself and other humans entirely free from sin, sickness, heartbreak, and death. His design allows people to dwell in His Presence as they bring glory to God through personal relationships and fulfilling their roles on the earth. The entire Creation and design for creation reveals the LORD's eternal glory.

While Genesis 1 provides readers with an overview of creation, Genesis 2 focuses on the creation of Adam and Eve. Genesis 2 is a further explanation of Genesis 1:27, "So God created man in His own image, in the image of God He created him; male and female He created them." It is in the second chapter of Genesis that we see the LORD's personal name: YHWH (Gen. 2:4). As mentioned before, the use of YHWH denotes God's personal and relational name. The use of YHWH would be like calling a close family member or friend by their first name. It is noteworthy that the first use of YHWH is in correlation with His creation of the heavens and earth. He is the Eternal Creator. Over the next two days, you will be studying God's design for Creation, specifically mankind, as described in Genesis 2 and then His New Creation which restores all that was cursed by man's sin according to Revelation 21-22. As you study, ask YHWH Elohim to reveal to you the depths of His identity as the Creator that has been and always will be.

READ GENESIS 2:4-17.
Describe the way in which God created man in your own words.

The word "formed" in verse 7 is the Hebrew word "yatsar." This same word is used in Isaiah 64:8. How does Isaiah 64:8 give you a deeper understanding of what it means to be formed by God?

READ 1 CORINTHIANS 15:45-49.
What are the differences between the first Adam and the last Adam (Jesus Christ)?

Describe the Garden of Eden in which Adam was placed.

What was Adam's God-given purpose within the Garden of Eden?

Note: The words "work" and "keep" used in Genesis 2:15 are the same words used in the description of the role of the priests that were to "minister" and "guard" in the LORD's temple.

READ NUMBERS 3:7-8 AND NUMBERS 18:7.
What similarities do you find between the Garden and the Temple?

What similarities do you find between the work given to Adam and the work given to the priests?

What is God's view of work?

How are you challenged to view the work in which God has entrusted you? (See also, Eccles. 5:19.)

Why do you think God put the tree of the knowledge of good and evil within the garden and then forbid Adam from eating its fruit? (See also, John 14:15.)

READ GENESIS 2:18-25.
What additional role did YHWH Elohim give to Adam and how does this role reflect His purpose for man in Genesis 1:28?

In Paradise, God states that something is "not good" (Gen. 2:18). How does the Eternal Creator respond to what He identifies as "not good?"

The word for "helper" in Genesis 4:18 is used in Psalm 33:20, 70:5, and 111:9-12. How do these verses help the reader understand the role of the woman as the "helper?"

How might these verses assist in explaining the value of a woman according to God's design?

According to Genesis 2:24-25, what was YHWH Elohim's perfect design for human relationships?

Special Note: Genesis 3 describes the fall of mankind as they willfully rebel against the commands of God and suffer the consequences for their sins. Due to the curse upon mankind (and consequently, the earth), the law of sin and death reigned within the hearts and lives of all image-bearers. Jesus, who was with YHWH in the beginning, took on human form and died as the atoning sacrifice for mankind. Redemption was a part of God's plan for humans. Ultimately, YHWH Elohim's plan is to create a new heaven and earth with no darkness and eternal holiness for all who put their faith and trust in the atoning work of Jesus Christ. It is in this new heaven and new earth that those who are "in Christ" will enjoy His presence forever.

Review YHWH Shammah (The LORD Is There), Day 6 and 7, The New Jerusalem.

READ REVELATION 21:1-8.
Describe the new cosmos that is created by YHWH Elohim. How is this new creation a fulfillment of prophesy? (See also, Isa. 65:17-18 and 66:22.)

Although the first creation was not destined to last, make a list of all of the words and phrases that point to the eternal nature of the new creation.

Special Note: Jesus declares, "I am making all things new" (Rev. 21:5).

READ ROMANS 7:21-25.
In what way will God's people be made spiritually and morally new?

In what way will God's people be made physically and bodily new? (See also, Phil. 3:20-21.)

In what way will be creation be made new? (See also, Rom. 8:21.)

What evidence of YHWH Elohim, the Eternal
Creator, do you find in this passage?

READ REVELATION 21:9-26 - 22:5.
What aspects of the New Jerusalem stand out to you?

Do you find any similarities between the
Garden of Eden and the New Jerusalem?

What does it mean to you that the new heaven
and the new earth will last "forever and ever?"

The creation stories in Genesis 1 and Revelation 21-22 act as bookends to an unfathomable story of redemption. Before He ever created, YHWH had a plan. YHWH Elohim created the heavens and the earth, and He called them good. In the beginning He revealed His nature as having supreme authority and creative power. He set Himself apart as the only One who can call into existence humans, animals, and things from nothing. He revealed His glory in His creation, yet He knew that given freewill, mankind would fall. God allowed humans freewill knowing that it would result in YHWH Elohim hanging and dying on a cross. God allowed humans freewill knowing that they would love their sin; therefore, death, destruction, and heartache would be a part of their lives. YHWH is not a puppet-master, and we are not His puppets. As mankind reaped and continues to reap the consequences of rebellion against the Eternal Creator, creation groaned and continues to groan as it awaits its healing (Rom. 8:22).

In the beginning and in the current evil age, Satan was and is allowed to tempt. In the end, Satan will be destroyed in the lake of fire as the saints enjoy perfect fellowship with the Eternal Creator in the new heaven and new earth. The creation in the beginning was not destined by God to last, but the creation at the end will continue forever and ever. YHWH Elohim is able to "make all things new" (Rev. 21:5). Because He is eternal in nature, He makes the new heavens, new earth, and individuals eternal as they enjoy His presence and intimacy in the New Jerusalem as Adam and Eve experienced in the Garden of Eden before the corruption of sin. Today, thank YHWH Elohim for not abandoning creation to its depravity. Thank Him for choosing to redeem His people so that they can partake in the restoration to come. As you apply this passage to your life, take note of the truth that YHWH Elohim chose to create you knowing in advance every way you would rebel against Himself. He didn't just create you with your lifespan on earth in mind; rather, if you are in Christ, He foreknew and predestined before the foundation of the earth that you would be called, justified, conformed into the image of Jesus, and glorified for all eternity with Himself in the New Heaven (Rom. 8:29-30). Worship YHWH Elohim today!

WEDNESDAY AND THURSDAY (DAY 3 AND 4): THE LORD OUR MAKER: YHWH HOSEENU

Psalm 95 is the only passage that contains the name of God: YHWH Hoseenu. This name is translated into English as the LORD Our Maker. The authorship of this song of praise is given to King David by the author of Hebrews in Hebrews 4:7. The beginning and middle of the psalm is spent exalting and praising God's leadership and might when compared to all other gods. The people are called to recognize the blessings that they experience by being under the kingship of YHWH. The second portion of the psalm is a warning to steer clear from rebelling against YHWH due to hard hearts. They are warned of YHWH's wrath and authority to deny people His presence forever.

David mentions two places in which the Israelites hardened their hearts against the LORD Our Maker: Meribah and Massa. In both accounts, the Israelites grumbled against Moses due to their perceived lack of water in the wilderness. Instead of crying out to the LORD in faith as their Creator who had the power to create water out of nothing, they spoke against God and accused Him of wrongdoing. Instead of worshipping the Maker, they pridefully judged Him as guilty of sin despite being eyewitnesses to His power on their behalf time and time again. David brings up the past history of the nation of Israel to prophetically warn His people from hardening their hearts against the One who is Maker and LORD. As you study, ask the LORD to help you come into His presence with thanksgiving for all that He has done in the past, and ask Him to protect you from the evil one who whispers lies as he seeks to harden your heart against YHWH Hoseenu whenever circumstances do not match your expectations. The enemy, Satan, will always lie about the character of YHWH. He did so in the Garden of Eden as He planted suspicions in Eve's heart that the LORD was withholding good from both her and Adam whenever He commanded that they avoid eating from the tree of the Knowledge of Good and Evil (Gen. 3), and He lied to the Israelites and tempted them to believe that YHWH wouldn't provide water in the wilderness. Take up the sword of the Spirit, the Word of God (Eph. 6:17-18), by memorizing Scripture as the enemy tempts you to doubt or question the attributes of the LORD so that your heart does not become hardened toward your Maker.

READ PSALM 95:1-7A.
What are the people of God
encouraged to do in verses 1-2?

Write down every name ascribed to God in this passage.

Write down every description, ability, and action of God in this passage.

What should be our response to the LORD's names, descriptions, abilities, and actions?

What descriptions do you find of God's people within this passage?

What specific verses and phrases point to the LORD's creative power?

READ PSALM 95:7B-11.

Explain the Israelites' hardness of hearts in Meribah and Massah in the wilderness? (Read Exodus 17:1-7.)

Special Note: Psalm 95 is quoted throughout Hebrews 3 and 4.

According to Hebrews 3:13, what is one cause of hearts becoming hard?

According to Hebrews 4:15-16, how can we keep from developing a hard heart due to sin?

How did the Israelites put the LORD to the test at Meribah and Massah? (Read Exod. 17:1-7.)

According to the following verses, what is the LORD's stance on putting Him to the test: Matthew 5:4-7, Luke 11:29, 1 Corinthians 10:9-11.

David prophetically writes the words of the LORD, "When your fathers put me to the test and put me to proof, though they had seen my work" in verse 9. According to Romans 1:18-20, what works have all of mankind seen?

What does His work reveal about His attributes and character?

Read Numbers 14:21-35 and explain the history mentioned in Psalm 95:10-11.

> Can people enter into the LORD's rest today? If so,
> what does this look like in the life of a believer still on
> the earth? (See also, Heb. 4:1-2, 9-11, and Eph. 2:8-9.)

The focus of the first half of Psalm 95 is on praising the LORD: He is ascribed names such as "great King above all gods" and "The LORD Our Maker." He is given descriptions such as "the rock of our salvation," and His creative works are listed. Readers find reference to His role as YHWH Raah, the LORD is Our Shepherd, as the congregation celebrates the fact that they are "sheep of His pasture." When the congregation beholds YHWH Hoseenu's creative ability in making the depths of the earth, the heights of the mountains, the sea, and the dry land, the right response is worshipping Him in humility. As we consider the works of His hands, we are to bow down before Him as the great King above all gods. No other god has or ever will create. In recognizing how worthy the LORD is of singing, thanksgiving, joyful noises, songs of praise, and so on, the people guard against becoming hard of heart toward their Maker. We must learn to mediate upon His attributes and praise Him for His acts as the adversary, the Devil, prowls around looking to harden the people of God.

At Meribah and Massah, the Israelites failed to recount the past deeds of YHWH Hoseenu. In the sight of Israel, God had created blood in the place of water, an abundance of frogs and flies, and hailstones as He inflicted plagues upon the Egyptians for the purpose of delivering Israel out of slavery. He did this while sparing the land of Goshen where the people of Israel were located (Exod. 17:26). He created dry land for the Israelites to safely walk on as He parted the Red Sea. He created and sent bread from Heaven to feed His people. He transformed bitter waters into sweet waters for His people to drink. Despite these displays of creative power, the Israelites tested the LORD due to their thirst at Massah and Meribah saying, "Is the LORD among us or not" (Exod. 17:7)? Such a question was like saying, "Is God even real? Does He even care?" They accused Him of absence, lack of power, and wrongdoing by their testing and quarreling.

Such sins are not reserved for just the Israelites who wandered in the wilderness. David draws upon Israel's history to implore the congregation to remember the LORD Our Maker's work; therefore, not hardening their hearts, putting Him to the test, and demanding proof of His existence. David writes from the LORD's perspective, "I loathed that generation" (Ps. 95:10), because they were people that went astray in their hearts and didn't know His ways. The "heart" refers to the entirety of a person's emotions, thoughts, and decisions. The Israelites that provoked God at Massah and Meribah went astray from God with all of their emotions, thoughts, and decisions and paid little regard to His ways. Such behavior hinders people from entering into the LORD's rest and peace. Today, ask the LORD Our Maker to remind you of His mighty works. Repent for ways in which you have hardened your heart and strayed from His ways. Take time to worship Him with songs of praise — for He is your Maker.

FRIDAY (DAY 5): REFLECTION

Respond to the reflection questions below prayerfully and honestly.

Using your notes from the past week of study, write down aspects of the LORD's character. Which aspects mean the most to you? Explain your answer.

In what ways do you personally relate to the Israelites' hardness of hearts? Write a prayer of confession and repentance.

> Can you identify one or two lies that the enemy feeds you about the character and nature of YHWH? Write down the lie and research a Scripture to memorize to combat the enemy's scheme to harden your heart against your Maker.

MONDAY AND TUESDAY (DAY 6 AND 7): JESUS AS CREATOR

Creative power belongs to God alone. He is the only Eternal Creator. In John 10:30, Jesus declares, "I and the Father are one." Jesus makes Himself equal with God and further proves that He is God by His creative miracles while He walked the earth as both man and God. Jesus revealed God to humanity in that He was the exact representation of His nature on the earth (Heb. 1:3). Jesus even used God's personal name revealed to Moses through the burning bush (Exod. 3:14) to refer to Himself whenever the Roman soldiers, officers, chief priests, and Pharisees came to arrest Him in the middle of the night. The crowd of people that sought to arrest Jesus stated that they were looking for "Jesus of Nazareth." Jesus answered them, "I AM He" which caused the crowd to draw back and involuntarily fall to the ground (John 18:3-6). Through this statement, among others throughout His ministry, Jesus claimed to be I AM WHO I AM which corresponds to the four Hebrew consonants that make God's personal name: YHWH. Jesus claimed to be the self-existent, uncreated, immutable God. Such a claim either makes Jesus a raving lunatic or exactly who He said: YHWH.

Over the next two days, you will study passages in which Jesus performed creative miracles that reveal His identity as YHWH and speak to the divine attribute of the LORD as Maker. In attaching Elohim and Hoseenu to the LORD's personal name, Moses and David were describing the very nature and character of the LORD — character that is infinite and unchangeable; therefore, since Jesus makes YHWH known, it is no surprise that He would show creative power throughout His ministry. Jesus didn't follow a special formula whenever He performed miracles; rather, He submitted Himself to the Father's will in obedience (John 6:38). His miracles often came from a place of compassion as Jesus was faced with a pressing need. When Jesus looked upon a distressed and dispirited crowd, He felt compassion for them because they were like sheep without a Shepherd (Matt. 9:36). Before healing the sick, it's often recorded that He "felt compassion for them" (Matt. 14:14). Today, praise the Eternal Creator for His power and compassion that led to many creative miracles throughout His time on earth. Consider, how can you be led by compassion today?

READ JOHN 2:1-12.

What was the problem or need at the Wedding in Cana?

How does Jesus' address this problem?

Explain how this miracle is evidence of Jesus' deity and power as Creator?

According to this passage, what was the purpose of this miracle?

READ JOHN 5:1-18
Who was at the Bethesda pool and why were they there?

Describe the man in which Jesus took particular interest.

What happens to one's body after being an invalid for 38 years?

How did Jesus heal the invalid?

What creating within the invalid's body had to occur in order for him to have been able to take up his bed and walk?

What was the result of this miracle?

READ JOHN 6:1-15.
What was the need that Jesus identified?

What resources were already available to feed the crowd?

What did Jesus do to address the need?

How is this miracle evidence of Jesus power as Eternal Creator?

What was the result of this miracle?

READ JOHN 11:38 - 44.
How long had the man, Lazarus, been dead?

How did Jesus restore life to Lazarus?

How is this miracle evidence of His creative power?

What was the purpose of this
miracle according to Jesus?

READ JOHN 18:1-11.
What did Simon Peter do? To whom did he do it?

What was Jesus' response? (See also, Luke 22:50-51.)

How does this miracle display Jesus'
authority as the LORD Our Maker?

What do you think might have been Malchus'
response to this undeserved healing?

Jesus' miracles ranged from creating bread, fish, and wine to completely restoring mutilated, maimed, and atrophied people. In Matthew 15, great crowds of lame, blind, crippled, and mute people were brought to Jesus for healing. He healed them all, and they were completely restored. The Greek word used for crippled in Matthew 15:30 is also translated as "maimed" or "mutilated" as seen in Matthew 18:8 and Mark 9:43. The implication is that Jesus created new limbs and other body parts — body parts that might have been cut off due to sinful behavior since the law commanded an eye for an eye, a hand for a hand, a foot for a foot, and a tooth for a tooth (Exod. 21:24). Some body parts might have been lost as a result of sickness or injury. Whatever the case, someone who was disabled wasn't awarded government financial help during the Biblical age; they were often sentenced to lives of poverty and struggle. As Jesus restored physical bodies, He met their needs emotionally and financially as well.

There is no other explanation for the amazing miracles that Jesus performed other than the fact that He truly was with God in the beginning as Creator and that all things were made by Him and through Him. In Him is both life and restoration. (John 1:1-3). It is amazing to consider that Jesus did many other signs that were not recorded in the Bible (John 20:30), so many miracles that "were every one of them to be written ... the world itself could not contain the books that would be written" (John 21:25). Today, mediate on Jesus' compassion. Are you faithfully reflecting the LORD's compassion in your day-to-day interactions? Secondly, recognize that Jesus was God in the flesh. Ask YHWH Elohim to set your heart on the truth that He is Creator of all, and all creation is dependent upon the Creator and Sustainer of the Universe. Trust Him today. Depend upon Him. "Is anything too hard for the LORD" (Exod. 18:14)?

WEDNESDAY AND THURSDAY (DAY 8 AND 9): NEW CREATIONS IN CHRIST

YHWH Hoseenu created mankind in His image and for a purpose. The purpose was and is to bring glory to Himself (Ps. 43:7) which is unselfish because it is in His name alone that men and women are saved. God showed His glory in creating the universe, then at the proper time, He created within a humble Jewish girl. God created Jesus as a single cell within Mary to grow and develop as the rest of mankind. God knitted together Jesus within her womb and formed His inmost parts. Then Jesus, though He was God, died on the cross for the forgiveness of sins so that all who believe could be created anew in Christ. Jesus called the process of becoming a new creation being "born again." This rebirth did not come from a mother's womb but the Spirit of God — the same Spirit that hovered over the deep in the beginning (John 3:3,5; Gen. 1:2). Without this new birth, it is impossible to enter the Kingdom of God.

The Apostle Paul explains this new creation in a different way as he writes that Christians "have put off the old self with its practices and have put on the new self, which is being renewed in the knowledge after the image of its creator" (Col. 3:9-10). The LORD, through the prophet Ezekiel, explained how Christians become new creations in Christ by declaring "And I will give them one heart, and a new spirit I will put within them. I will remove the heart of stone from their flesh and give them a heart of flesh, that they may walk in My statutes and keep My rules and obey them. And they shall be my people, and I will be their God" (Ezek. 11:19-20). Such a proclamation awards YHWH the credit for such an act of creation within a person's inner self.

The same creative, authoritative power that YHWH Elohim displayed as He created the heavens and the earth is seen as He causes one to become "born again" in Himself so that they die to their old life and walk with a new nature and the imputed righteousness of Christ. The change within a human heart is just as powerful a miracle as the creation of mankind in the beginning. Just as humans lack the power to create the heavens, earth, and all that is in the earth, humans lack the power to create new hearts within themselves. Throughout the next two days, you will read select passages that describe how a believer becomes a new creation in Christ through His power. As you study, bear in mind that the Supreme Creator of the universe subjected Himself to becoming a single cell inside of a young woman only to grow up and die a humiliating and excruciating death on a cross to redeem image-bearers that whole-heartedly hated and reject YHWH. His humility and love are absolutely scandalous! Ask the LORD Our Maker to cultivate love in your heart as you study His divine plan to make you new — especially considering the great lengths through which the Creator went to make it possible for you to be created anew in Christ.

READ 2 CORINTHIANS 5:14-21.
What has Christ's death accomplished for the believer? (See also, Rom. 3:21-26.)

What happens to one's old life when they are in Christ? (See also, Gal. 2:20.)

How does Christ's life free believers to walk in new life? (See also, Rom. 6:1-14 and Tit. 2:11-14.)

In your own words, explain what it means to become a new creation in Christ. (See also, Ezek. 36:35-37, Eph. 2:22-24, John 3:3.)

According to verse 18, who is responsible for making new creations out of humans? (See also, 2 Cor. 3:18, John 1:12-13.)

What is a person's responsibility after becoming a new creation in Christ? (See also, Col. 3:3-17.)

Look up a definition for "reconciliation" and write it below. According to the passage, what is the biblical definition of reconciliation? How are they similar? How are they different?

Using verses 18 and 20, what two job descriptions are assigned to those that have been justified before God?

Write verse 21. What does it mean that we "become the righteousness of God?" (See also, Rom. 3:21-22, 5:18-19, 1 Cor. 1:30, 2 Cor. 5:17, 19.)

Special Note: Paul was addressing the fact that some were teaching that believers must be circumcised in order to be truly saved from the wrath of God and enter into Heaven.

READ GALATIANS 6:13-16.
What counts to the LORD?

What does not count?

READ EPHESIANS 2:8-10.
Described how one is saved?

Whose workmanship are we?

What does it mean that you have been "created in Christ Jesus?" (Refer to questions and Scriptures used throughout the past two days of study.)

What is the purpose of being "created in Christ Jesus?"

What works has God prepared
for you to walk in today?

The same YHWH Hoseenu who fearfully and wonderfully made mankind (Ps. 139:14) is responsible for remaking them in Himself. Men and women do not have the power or the will to remove their own heart of stone and replace it with a heart that beats and longs for obedience to God's commands and communion with the Father. Humans do not have the ability or authority to rebirth themselves into new creations that reflect the attributes of YHWH. Without God's divine, irresistible initiative it would be impossible for humans to be justified and reconciled to the Maker of all. As we study the Scriptures surrounding becoming new creations in Christ, it is clear that all glory belongs to God. Before we take the credit for our faith or works, we must remember that we are but clay and YHWH Elohim is the potter (Isa. 64:8). We are His workmanship, and we have been created in Christ Jesus for the purpose of good works (Eph. 2:10). If one is truly in Christ, his or her old self has passed away and his or her new self has come. It is YHWH Hoseenu who accomplishes this creation miracle within the believer, but the Christian is not without responsibility.

Christians are urged to carry out the ministry of reconciliation and represent Christ to others as His ambassadors. They are tasked with spreading the message of reconciliation: there is a way to be made right with God through Jesus' atoning death on the cross. Christians, the very workmanship of YHWH Hoseenu, are created new in Christ for the purpose of walking in good works that have been prepared in advanced by

God (Eph. 2:10). Because Christians have died to their old way of living and been given new life in Christ, they are commanded to put off the ways of the old self — anything that is earthly and contrary to the image of God. Because any new creation in Christ is God's chosen, holy, and beloved (Col. 3:12), they are to put on His character through His power. Praise YHWH Elohim for His ability to make a person completely new. Praise YHWH Hoseenu for His power to remake His creation as He conforms men and women into the image of Jesus.

FRIDAY (DAY 10): REFLECTION

Complete the following reflection questions prayerfully and honestly.

Consider the fact that if you have come to saving faith in Jesus Christ's atonement for your sins and resurrection and have followed Him as the Lord of your life, you are made a new creation in Him. Since following Jesus, what old things have passed away?

What new things have come (2 Cor. 5:17)?

What aspects of your old self have you put off (Colossians 3:9)?

What aspects of your new self have you put on (Ephesians 4:24)?

If you are a new creation, you have been given the ministry of reconciliation and are considered an ambassador for God Himself while on the earth. Take time to evaluate how seriously you have taken this God-given responsibility. List ways in which you can practically participate in the ministry of reconciliation and represent Christ to the world.

BIBLIOGRAPHY

ESV Study Bible: English Standard Version. Wheaton, IL: Crossway, 2011.

ABOUT THE AUTHOR BIOGRAPHY

Laura Ackley has been a Christian since 2004 and considers Jesus both her first love and the joy of her life. She earned a master's degree in Curriculum and Instruction and is passionate about creating Bible study curriculum for the glory of God. She is a wife to her high school sweetheart, Scott Ackley, and a mother of two children — Kylie and Levi. She served as an elementary public educator for five years before transitioning to life as a stay-at-home mom. In 2020, Laura opened a private Christian Pre-Kindergarten named Mrs. Ackley's Adventure School in which she prepares students for kindergarten through hands-on, project-based learning experiences. Within her local church, she serves as a worship leader, youth leader, and Bible teacher, and enjoys coordinating community outreach events. Her hobbies include hiking, camping, animals, social gatherings, singing, reading, writing, public speaking, and coffee.

ENDORSEMENT

This study brings a fresh perspective to the subject of the character and attributes of God. It draws the reader toward a deeper knowledge of the true God as revealed in Scripture. It strikes the right balance between insightful scholarship and devotional application. The author does an excellent job in linking the Old Testament foundation to the New Testament fulfillment in Jesus Christ.

Dr. Darren Heil